WOLVES OF THE WORLD

Printed in China

04   05   06   07   08   5   4   3   2   1

Library of Congress Cataloging-in-Publication Data

Fuller, T.K.
        Wolves of the world / Todd K. Fuller.
            p. cm.
        Includes bibliographical references and index.
        ISBN 0-89658-640-5
        1. Wolves. 1. Title.
        QL737.C22F85 2004
        599.773-dc22
                                            2003018736

Published by Voyageur Press, Inc.
123 North Second Street, P.O. Box 338, Stillwater, MN 55082 U.S.A.
651-430-2210, fax 651-430-2211
books@voyageurpress.com
www.voyageurpress.com

Distributed in Canada by Raincoast Books, 9050 Shaughnessy Street, Vancouver, B.C. V6P 6E5

Educators, fundraisers, premium and gift buyers, publicists, and marketing managers:
Looking for creative products and new sales ideas? Voyageur Press books are available at special discounts when purchased in quantities, and special editions can be created to your specifications. For details contact the marketing department at 800-888-9653.

Photography © 2004 by:

Front Cover © Jorge Sierra
Back Cover © Lisa & Mike Husar/Team Husar
Page 1 © Tim Fitzharris
Page 3 © Staffan Widstrand
Page 4 © Lisa & Mike Husar/Team Husar
Page 6 © Lisa & Mike Husar/Team Husar
Page 8 © Staffan Widstrand
Page 10 © Martin Harvey/NHPA
Page 13 © Erwin & Peggy Bauer
Page 14L © Art Wolfe
Page 14R © Art Wolfe
Page 17 © Martin Harvey/NHPA
Page 19 © Tim Fitzharris
Page 20 © Staffan Widstrand
Page 23 © Lisa & Mike Husar/Team Husar
Page 24 © Jim Brandenburg/Minden
Page 26 © Tom Walker
Page 29 © Tim Fitzharris
Page 30 © Jim Brandenburg/Minden
Page 33 © Jim Brandenburg/Minden
Page 34 © Lisa & Mike Husar/Team Husar
Page 37 © Joanna Van Gruisen/Ardea
Page 39 © Tim Fitzharris

Page 40 © Art Wolfe
Page 43 © Jim Brandenburg/Minden
Page 44 © Jim Brandenburg/Minden
Page 47 © Jim Brandenburg/Minden
Page 49 © Robert D Franz
Page 50 © Kennan Ward
Page 51 © Kennan Ward
Page 53 © Erwin & Peggy Bauer
Page 54 © Konrad Wothe
Page 59 © Lisa & Mike Husar/Team Husar
Page 60 © Lisa & Mike Husar/Team Husar
Page 65 © Kennan Ward
Page 66 © Staffan Widstrand
Page 69 © Lisa & Mike Husar/Team Husar
Page 70 © Staffan Widstrand
Page 73 © Jorge Sierra
Page 74 © Art Wolfe
Page 77 © Erwin & Peggy Bauer
Page 79 © Lisa & Mike Husar/Team Husar
Page 80 © Lisa & Mike Husar/Team Husar
Page 83 © Jorge Sierra
Page 84 © Staffan Widstrand
Page 87 © Jim Brandenburg/Minden

Page 88 © Martin Grosnick/Ardea
Page 91 © Henry Ausloos/NHPA
Page 92 © Tom Walker
Page 95 © Jim Brandenburg/Minden
Page 96 © Lisa & Mike Husar/Team Husar
Page 98 © Jim Brandenburg/Minden
Page 100 © Michael Mauro/Minden
Page 103 © Konrad Wothe
Page 104 © Tim Fitzharris
Page 107 © Jorge Sierra
Page 108 © Staffan Widstrand
Page 113 © Staffan Widstrand
Page 114 © Douglas W. Smith & Debra Guernsey
Yellowstone National Park. USA
Page 115 © Art Wolfe
Page 117 © Lisa & Mike Husar/Team Husar
Page 118 © Jorge Sierra
Page 121 © Jim Brandenburg/Minden
Page 123 © Jorge Sierra
Page 124 © Staffan Widstrand
Page 125 © Jim Brandenburg/Minden
Page 127 © Jim Brandenburg/Minden
Page 130 © Peter Weimann/Still Pictures
Page 131 © Daniel Cox/OSF

WOLVES OF THE WORLD

Todd K. Fuller

Foreword by Luigi Boitani

Voyageur Press

Contents

Foreword

One of the fascinations of studying wolves is that, in spite of several thousands of scientific publications on their biology and management, we continue to learn and gain new insights from every new study of wolves. Their biological flexibility is the main reason for their phenomenal resilience to some of the most intense extermination campaigns ever launched by man against an animal species.

From Arctic tundra to the deserts of Mongolia and Saudi Arabia, wolves respond to the great variety of environments with a wide range of functional adaptations. Wolves are so diverse throughout their range that studying them in Alaska or in India can yield very different results; the fundamental ecological and behavioral patterns are obviously the same, but their interactions with different prey species and habitats create a great diversity of ecological and behavioral solutions. Because of this variation we must be careful in generalising about wolves, as well as in extrapolating data to areas different from where they were originally collected.

Ecological and behavioral flexibility is the most fascinating aspect of wolf biology and what makes the wolf a truly special animal, yet this is also the most difficult aspect to be correctly presented in a popular book on wolves. Of the many wolf books in all kinds of languages, only a handful are able to avoid the pitfalls that reduce the complexity of wolf biology to an easy and unnatural cliché. This beautiful study by Todd K. Fuller is one of those rare books which tells the true story of the wolf, and this is certainly due to the fact that Todd, as well as being a good writer, is also an excellent wolf biologist with many years spent in the field watching, handling, and studying wolves.

Writing a popular text on wolves is not an easy task because many people don't realize that much of what they have already learned about wolves is wrong. In fact a large portion of the popular knowledge on wolves is still based on legends, tales, and beliefs that have been created by traditional societies throughout the centuries. Early human societies had firm roots in their natural environment, and in these cultures wolves were usually respected and considered a positive influence. It was not until the Middle Ages that the image of the wolf changed dramatically and the "bad wolf" appeared for the first time. People began to believe that wolves possessed dark supernatural powers. Many of these beliefs still persist to this day.

Our increasingly urbanized lifestyles can leave less and less opportunity to experience the rhythms and patterns of nature. Today, new types of beliefs, symbols and meanings have become associated with the wolf. They are now symbols of wilderness, of ecosystem health, and of conservation battles. In many ways the wolf is being idealized and mythologized with the same emotional intensity as it was when it was impugned. However, such rarefication does not necessarily form the best basis to create new and durable solutions for wolf conservation. This book will inform you with scientific accuracy and unique field experiences why wolves are special animals. However, the issue of wolf conservation ultimately relies on our changing attitudes and action. The real challenge for long term sustainable wolf conservation is in learning how to coexist with wolves, not in segregating them in the ever rarer protected areas. However, this may require some compromise on both sides, wolf and human.

Luigi Boitani, Professor, University of Rome "La Sapienza"

Wolves are among the most studied animals in the world. They are, extremely adaptable, and wolf ecology varies tremendously depending on whether they live in Alaska or India. Because of wolves' varied interactions with humans, their conservation is an ongoing challenge.

Preface

On a cold, still Minnesota night in December 1972, I first heard wolves howl. I had probably heard a "wolf howl" as a background sound on some television show when I was younger, but this was the real thing and I was awestruck. I was deep in the woods near the Canadian border, out on a snow-covered logging road with Dave Mech, at the time already a famous wolf biologist. Dave had published his Ph.D. research on the wolves of Isle Royale, Michigan in 1966. By 1968 he was a U.S. Fish and Wildlife Service scientist starting up a wolf radio-telemetry study in the last part of the lower 48 states that still had a resident wolf population. That wolves were being considered one of the first official endangered species in the country made his efforts all the more promising. His classic 1970 book, *The Wolf*, was by far the most complete and up-to-date synthesis available for any carnivore species, and he is today still the world's leading authority on wolves.

In 1972, I was a young and relatively naïve student at the University of California at Davis, eager to find out more about wildlife biology, my chosen major. Luckily, my older brother, Mark, was a Ph.D. student at the University of Minnesota using radio telemetry to study birds of prey. Having common interests and research approaches, he had met and talked with Dave, and subsequently arranged a trip to Dave's study area for us during the Christmas holiday. We drove north from the Twin Cities to Ely, a town that, in summer, is the gateway to the Boundary Waters Wilderness Area. This vast, isolated area extending into southern Ontario was dotted with lakes and drained by many streams and rivers. The day was bright and clear when Dave took us up in the single-engine aircraft used to track his radio-collared wolves. Below was a rolling landscape of snow and ice and coniferous trees, and when we finally did see the wolves, they appeared as balls of fur curled up in the snow.

Because the wolves were less than a mile from the nearest drivable trail, and because both the temperature and wind were dropping, Dave wanted to go out after dinner and see if we could get the wolves to howl. Wolves actually are more likely to respond to human 'howls' than to tape-recordings of actual wolf howls, and conditions that night were just about perfect for receiving a reply. After a half-hour drive and a quick check of the radio receiver just to make sure the wolves had stayed put, we quietly prepared to give a "group" howl – one that would mimic a typical pack sing-a-long, with a variety of intermingling, mournful notes that purposefully avoided any sense of harmony. Sure enough, after a 5-second pause that seemed much longer, the pack howled back. They howled for what I thought was a long time, and none of us moved or made a sound. It was certainly a song of the wild; a heart-tugging, adrenalin-releasing sound that to this day makes me pause when I recall it.

Since that night, I have heard and elicited wolf howls in other parts of Minnesota, in northern Alberta, Canada, and even in the Gobi Desert of Mongolia. I have trapped, measured, and sampled them. I have watched wolves, mostly from airplanes, go about many of their daily routines, and have seen the remains of their activities in a variety of forms. Dens, scats, kills, tracks all provide insights that I have found interesting and useful. In addition to my early, mostly field interactions with wolves, I also have spent considerable time in an office in front of a pad of paper or a computer. In formal and informal meetings with a variety of people we have tried to figure out how many wolves were around, and how many could be around in the future. I have spent a lot of time thinking about how wolves and humans might continue to co-exist. A shared future, however, is not guaranteed, largely because of the deeply held feelings and beliefs, both positive and negative that wolves evoke in humans.

Taxonomy:
What is a Wolf?

When most of us imagine a wolf, we think correctly of the large, dog-like animal that lives (or did live) throughout the northern hemisphere and often travels together with others of its kind. They are locally called gray wolves, timber wolves, steppe wolves, and sometimes Arctic wolves or tundra wolves, but they are all the same species.

There are, however, other dog-like animals, known scientifically as canids, which are also called wolves, but usually only with a modifying descriptor in front of the name. These include the closely related and widely ranging North American coyote, sometimes referred to as a brush wolf; the red wolf of southeastern North America, once wide-spread but now recovering in one location in the wild only through intensive re-establishment efforts; the Ethiopian wolf from Africa, formerly known as the Simien jackal; the African wild dog, or painted wolf; the maned wolf of South America, often described as a big red fox on stilts; and the culpeo zorro, also from South America, locally called the Andean wolf. Though evolutionarily related to wolves in one way or another, these are all separate, identifiable species of canids that live in their own ways. They are not what we are referring to when we talk, in general, about wolves.

We know wolves are wolves from the way they look, and the ways they behave with each other and with other species. They were named scientifically in the 18th century by the Swedish professor, physician, and naturalist, Carolus Linneaus, the "father" of modern scientific nomenclature, referred to as binomial classification. Scientists and the general public alike recognized the close affinity of wolves and domestic dogs; thus Linneaus' Latin name designation, *Canis lupus*, appropriately enough means "wolf dog".

Despite the tremendous variation in the size and color of wolves throughout their range, and even some variability in their social behavior (see Chapters 3 and 5, respectively), wolves have long been recognized as a single species through physical or morphological characteristics, particularly features of their skulls. These features are also used to investigate their ancestry by measuring fossil or otherwise preserved skulls of wolves living long ago. More recently, wolves have been studied via their biochemistry and genetics, including chromosome, enzyme, and molecular (DNA) analyses. These assessments not only allow us to investigate living or recently living wolves, but also those preserved in the permafrost of the arctic for up to 50,000 years.

Wolf Ancestry

So how did wolves come to be? Fossils indicate that the kind of canid we label with the genus name *Canis* first developed about 6 million years ago. Previously, there had been fox-like canids, as well as a group of very large and ponderous canids called the Borophaginae that seemed to be dying out about that time. The evolution of the *Canis* group started with development of small forms something like jackals, and by 3 million years ago they occurred in both the Old World and North America, with a separate group of canids evolving in South America. By about 2 million years ago some of these *Canis* split into more wolf-like and more coyote-like animals. The wolf-like canids became larger about 800,000 years ago and split again into two groups, one which would become the wolves we know today and the other which became the most widely known extinct canid, the dire wolf, scientifically named *Canis dirus*. Along these evolutionary pathways, during several hundreds of thousands of years and

This Ethiopian wolf pup is related to gray wolves, but is a separate species in the group known scientifically as canids.

across much of the world, perhaps 7 or 8 species of "wolf" existed at one time or another. These other fossil wolf species, once found in both Eurasia and North America, are closely related to current wolves but have since become extinct, as well.

Dire wolves show up regularly in the fossil record beginning about 130,000 years ago. They may have originated from wolf ancestors living in more southern parts of the Americas, and then invaded much of temperate North America where they were common until about 8,000 years ago when the species became extinct. They varied in size from as little as 50 kg (110 lbs) to perhaps 90 kg (almost 200 lbs), the largest *Canis* species ever recorded. The best known specimens of dire wolves are from the Rancho La Brea tar pits in Southern California (actually in downtown Los Angeles). Relative to wolves, they had more massive heads, larger teeth, and relatively short legs. Although they were not found in northern parts of North America, and thus apparently were a warmer weather species, their fossils have been found together with completely distinctive specimens of gray wolves, red wolves, and coyotes. This canid guild was part of a huge, large mammal assemblage known as the North American late Pleistocene megafauna. This group included other carnivores such as grizzly and black bears, mountain lions, and the now extinct American cheetahs, lions, and short-faced bears. These predators fed on an amazing variety of large mammal prey including now extinct species such as horses, camels, and giant ground sloths.

Wolf Subspecies

Modern wolves likely began to develop as a species in North America, but seem to have migrated and then developed most fully in the Old World before reinvading North America in the late Pleistocene, some 100,000-150,000 years ago. At one time, wolves were, other than human beings, the most widely spread mammal species in the world. They lived, as they do today, from the high Arctic where winters have no sunshine, through boreal forest and temperate grasslands to arid subtropical deserts. They are, we shall see, a highly mobile and very adaptable species. This variation in distribution, along with their mobility, has led to groups of wolves that not only look and behave differently, but also to a complexity in evolutionary relationships.

The term "subspecies", in general, refers to geographic groupings of wolves that seem to have similar morphology or appearance, and thus presumably a similar ancestry. When people speak of "arctic wolves" in Greenland, or maybe "timber wolves" in Minnesota they are often referring to such geographic, or "subspecies", though the actual genetic relationship among such wolves may not be clear. Nevertheless there are, more specifically, several good reasons why such groupings actually occur in nature. First of all, there is inherent variation among individuals of a species that are geographically widespread. In many vertebrate animals there is a relationship between body mass and surface area that results in larger bodied animals being able to withstand lower temperatures, and relatively smaller bodied animals being better able to deal with heat. As mean annual temperatures decrease in going from the equator to the north, mean wolf body sizes increase. All else being equal, there would then be a constant increase in size, or a gradient in size with the smallest wolves in India or Mexico, and the largest in Siberia or Alaska. In general, this is the case. But ecological conditions aren't always equal. Aside from temperatures not always following a strict gradient because of mountains, lakes, coasts, and deserts, the prey of wolves also varies significantly. For the most part, wolves everywhere depend on large mammals, particularly hoofed ones, for most of their food (see Chapter 8 – Food). This means that in some areas they prey almost exclusively on small deer or gazelles that might weigh 30-40 kg (75-100 lbs), and in others they kill very large elk and moose, or even bison weighing 600 kg (1,320 lbs). Although wolves are able to kill prey as large or larger than themselves by hunting cooperatively (see Chapter 8 – Food), it helps, evolutionarily

Wolf "subspecies" are geographic groupings that seem to have similar morphology or appearance, and thus presumably a similar ancestry. Genetic analyses have confirmed that the wolves, such as this one, which once lived in Mexico and the southwestern United States and are now being reintroduced there, can reasonably be identified with the subspecies designation of "Mexican" wolf.

The endangered Red wolf (left) is a canid species closely related to gray wolves that originally occurred throughout the southeastern United States and is being reintroduced there. The Maned wolf (right) is only distantly related to gray wolves; it is found throughout the east-central portion of South America where it feeds on various plants and animals.

speaking, to be bigger if you are going to tackle big prey. As a result, wolves preying on large animals have evolved to be larger than those living where prey is small. Finally, the size of wolves in any given area depends on the competitors that live there, as well. Given a limited range of prey or an abundance of other medium- and large-size carnivores in an area, successful wolves will be those that can exploit a particular kind and size of prey most efficiently. Where there were larger carnivores, such as dire wolves, that might capture similar prey in a similar way, wolves there would evolve to a relatively smaller size than where dire wolves were not present. Thus there are a variety of factors affecting "optimal" size in a given area for wolves, and thus conditions under which subspecific differences might logically become evident.

Another factor affecting the development and distribution of subspecies, and in fact an essential part of such development, are physical barriers that would reduce or eliminate the opportunities for wolves of different subspecies to interbreed. These limits to genetic exchange, at least over the time that it might take to develop subspecific differences, include oceans, continental glaciers, extreme deserts, and perhaps high mountain ranges. When glaciers retreat or ocean levels lower or climates moderate in deserts, these barriers become less effective, and wolves of one subspecies may invade the area occupied by another. This is believed to have happened when the Bering land bridge between Asia and North America periodically allowed great faunal interchanges. When such changes occur, related but morphologically distinct subspecies were brought into contact, with a resulting reshuffling of genes and morphological characteristics based on adaptation to the local environment. It may also turn out, based on the vagaries of such continental-scale changes in barrier position, that one subspecies of wolf may compare most similarly to others that are found on the other side of the world, and not those found adjacent to them.

Today we seem to have about 13 subspecies of wolves in the world – 5 in North America and 8 in Eurasia. In the past, scientists have described a good many more subspecies – in the 1940s and 1950s taxonomists identified at least 24 in North America alone. A more recent assessment of both morphological and genetic data, along with a more conservative definition of a subspecies that reasonably reflects potential barriers and glacial histories, has resulted in the reduced number overall. Our understanding of subspeciation also has been muddled by the effects of widespread elimination of wolves by humans in recent times, and subsequent changes in distribution of closely related canids that sometimes interbreed with wolves (see below).

Living Relatives

Other *Canis* species currently occur throughout the world; some are more closely related to wolves than others. Though the evolutionary relationships of some of these species to wolves are clear, others are not well known because of conflicting results from morphological and genetic data analyses.

Three species of jackals exist, two of them only in Africa and the third in both Africa and Eurasia. These were early offshoots in the genus *Canis*, and are themselves fairly well differentiated genetically if not morphologically. All three species are relatively small, usually weighing about 6-15 kg (15-20 lbs). The side-striped jackal (*Canis adustus*) occurs throughout tropical Africa, usually in thickly wooded areas, but not in dry forests or rain forests. They live in pairs and eat mainly insects, rodents, and plant material. The black-backed jackal (*Canis mesomelas*), sometimes called the silver-backed jackal, is widespread in eastern and southern Africa, but these major populations are not connected. They live in a wide variety of habitats, from desert sands to savannah grasslands to suburbs, usually where rainfall is not so high. Black-backed jackals eat a variety of prey, including small ungulates like gazelle calves. They also live in pairs, but often young of the year remain with their parents and may help raise a new litter of pups. Finally, the golden jackal (*Canis aureus*) is found in northern and eastern Africa, but also in southeastern Europe east to Myanmar and Thailand in Southeast Asia. The golden is the only jackal that co-occurs with wolves in Asia. It lives in open country more than the other jackal species, and displaces them from such habitats where the species co-occur. Golden jackals live in pairs and sometimes have "helper" offspring, as well. Like the other jackal species, they are opportunistic foragers and eat fruits, invertebrates, small mammals, and carrion (i.e., meat scavenged from carcasses).

The Ethiopian wolf (*Canis simiensis*), formerly known as the Simien jackal, is most likely from the lineage of *Canis* leading to wolves and coyotes, rather than the one leading to jackals. It can be nearly as large (13-18 kg; 30-40 lbs) as wolves living in the nearby Arabian Peninsula, but has an isolated distribution in the mountains of Ethiopia in northeastern Africa. Ethiopian wolves live in packs of 2-12 paired and related individuals, and prey primarily on small and medium-sized rodents found in the moorlands at altitudes >3,000m (10,000 ft.).

Coyotes (*Canis latrans*) are a North American species that were found only in the western half of the continent 500 years ago, but today range from coast to coast and from Alaska to Costa Rica. They are usually half the size of sympatric (co-occurring) wolves, usually weighing 10-16 kg (22-35 lbs). They typically occur in mated pairs but, particularly where there is an abundance of food in the form of large ungulate carcasses, they also live in family groups or packs of 3-10. They occupy in all kinds of habitats, including suburbs, and are among the continent's most adaptable carnivore species. They are an opportunistic predator and eat small rodents, birds, newborn and older ungulates, insects, fruit, carrion, and garbage.

Red wolves (*Canis rufus*) were once the only *Canis* species living in the part of North America southeast of a line from Texas to Maine, but were virtually extirpated by humans. In the late 1970s, the last red wolves in the wild were brought into captivity and bred to a population of several hundred. In the mid-1980s, these captive animals were then re-introduced into the wild in North Carolina on the east coast of North America where about 125 range today. They weigh 20-40 kg (44-88 lbs) and live in pairs or packs of 3-10 throughout the forests and marshlands of their range. Red wolves prey mostly on deer, rabbits, and other mammals.

The specific circumstances concerning the origin of domestic dogs are not definitively known, but they are clearly descendents of wolves (and not jackals) and thus the canid most closely related to wolves. Whether they are a sub-species of wolf (i.e., *Canis lupus familiaris*) or a separately and recently evolved species of their own (i.e., *Canis familiaris*) is still up for debate.

Dogs are often considered the product of wolves domesticated by humans, either for pets, food, hunting companions, or even "living blankets". Alternatively, however, it seems likely that dogs evolved on their own perhaps 12,000-15,000 years ago when humans settled in villages and created new niche-providing food sources (i.e., refuse piles and garbage dumps). Some wolves may have taken advantage of this resource, and those able to tolerate and adapt to close proximity of humans developed into the dogs we know today (at least those most numerous ones not selectively bred by humans for many purposes that are now recognized as "breeds" by kennel clubs). Though we think of dogs most often as in the possession of, or at least dependent on, humans, some dogs do thrive completely on their own in the wilds of Australia (dingoes) and New Guinea (singing dogs), as well.

Hybridization

Because of their close evolutionary history, wolves, dogs, coyotes, and red wolves, although considered separate species, can interbreed and produce hybrid offspring; even jackals and dogs (purposefully put

The Ethiopian wolf, once known as the Simien jackal, has an isolated distribution at high altitudes in the mountains of northeastern Africa.

together) have been known to interbreed successfully. In fact, wolf-dog hybrids are commonly produced intentionally by humans for a variety of reasons (but usually as a result of human vanity — wolf-dogs are "cool" to own). Nevertheless, hybridization of these closely related canids does not usually occur under natural circumstances in the wild. Distributional and behavioral differences keep hybridization between species from happening, except under rare circumstances. There is, however, evidence that hybridization of some closely related canids has occurred in the recent past, and scientists are still struggling to identify the circumstances under which it happened.

In several of the most studied cases, the barriers preventing hybridization seem to have broken down under similar circumstances. That is, the population of one species (usually wolves) became so reduced and fragmented that individual animals were unable to find mates of their own species. As a result, they mated with a similar canid species living in the same area and produced a litter of pups.

For dogs and wolves, this probably has happened for centuries in some places. In Italy, for instance, persecuted and isolated wolves found mates in the numerous herding dogs traveling with flocks of livestock across the landscape. More recently in Ethiopia, some sub-populations of Ethiopian wolves have become so small, and sympatric domestic dog populations so high, that hybridization has occurred there, as well.

For wild canids in North America, much of the identified hybridization also seems to have been the result of our persecution of wolves. As European colonists extirpated wolves from portions of the eastern half of North America, coyotes from the West were able to begin to invade these areas. They moved both north and south of the Great Lakes, and those moving north apparently met up with the wolves at the southern fringes of wolf distribution in Canada and sometimes mated with them. Thus, coyote genes show up in wolves from Minnesota to Quebec. In addition, the coyotes in the northeastern U.S. are unusually large and likely are a result of wolf-coyote hybridization events of the past.

Simultaneously, coyotes moving east and south of the Great Lakes did not meet up with wolves, but rather came into contact with domestic dogs, producing what were called "coy-dogs". This phenomenon still occurs today (though rarely) where coyotes are newly arrived and/or heavily persecuted.

In the eastern and southeastern parts of the United States, red wolves were being extirpated by humans at nearly the same rate as were timber wolves in the north. The last red wolves in the wild were found along isolated portions of the coast of Texas, and were known to be interbreeding with coyotes that had moved in from the west. The last "pure" red wolves bred in captivity were released into the wild where no coyotes resided. Over a period of only 10 years or so, though, coyotes continued their invasion of the east and moved into the red wolf release area. Red wolf-coyote matings are now routine in this area, though intensive management of these hybrids is undertaken in order to build up the pure red wolf population to the extent that opportunities to mate with other red wolves is high.

Because of the hybridization potential, the taxonomic affiliations of some canids in the northeastern U.S. and southeastern Canada, in particular, remain unsettled. This confusion results from conflicting morphological and genetic information, and because the reconstruction of the history of canid movements in the area is poor. It is unlikely that under natural circumstances any of these hybridizations would have occurred to the extent that they have, but canids are a very adaptive, wide-ranging group, and have taken advantage of opportunities to mate whenever they occur. Further genetic investigations of canid relationships should clarify the historic and current taxonomy of wolves and their relatives in these areas.

Wolves are capable of hybridizing with both dogs and coyotes, and have done so in Europe and North America, respectively.

Morphology:
What do Wolves Look Like?

Physical Characteristics

Size

A newborn wolf pup would fit in your cupped hands; it weighs only about 0.5 kg (1.1 lb) and is darkly, finely furred. Its eyes are closed, its snout is short, and its tiny ears are still without much use. During the next several months, while being suckled with its littermates, it will grow very quickly and gain an average of about 1.2-1.5 kg (2.6-3.3 lb) per week. Then until it is about 6 months old, its growth rate will slow a bit (0.6-0.8 kg [1.3-1.7 lb] per week). Still, in the fall when 6 or 7 months old, a pup born the previous spring will be at least three quarters the weight of an adult and from a distance look about the same size. One 7-month-old male pup we caught in central Alberta in November weighed 43 kg (95 lbs), only about 5 kg (11 lbs) less than the average adult male wolf, and it wasn't until after it died (killed by other wolves, actually) that we could be certain that it was not older.

By the age of 1 year, most wolves have reached adult proportions in both skeletal size and weight. Although there is wide variation in wolf size over their geographic range, males are about 20% larger than females wherever wolves occur. In general, males measure about 150-200 cm (60-78 in) from tip of nose to tip of tail, and females measure about 140-185 cm (55-72 in); of this total length, the bushy tail accounts for about 35-55 cm (14-22 in). When standing, wolves are rather tall. Their shoulder height usually averages about 65-80 cm (26-32 in), but can reach 90 cm (35 in).

As with body size, wolf weights can vary considerably between areas, and may even vary within an area depending on environmental conditions. In general, adult male wolves average 43-48 kg (95-105 lb) or so, and females 36-42 kg (80-90 lb). The heaviest wolves live in northern areas of North America and Eurasia, but males weighing over 57 kg (125 lbs) are relatively rare. Still, a wolf weighing 79 kg (175 lb) has been recorded in Alaska. Sometimes, the weight of wolves may include what's in their stomach, and (as noted below) this may include meat, bones, fat and fur weighing up to 8 kg (18 lb). In general, wolves in lower latitudes are smaller than those farther north, especially those living in dry, desert regions such as in India or Saudi Arabia. Adult wolves in these areas may weigh only 18-20 kg (40-45 lb). This variation between wolves north and south is related both to the physics of keeping warm or cool, as well as average prey size. Remember that it is easier for large wolves to retain body heat, and for small wolves to get rid of excess heat. Also, large wolves are likely to be more successful killing very large prey such as moose or bison than are small wolves.

Within any one area, wolf weights may vary as much as 20% within a sex. This variation may have some genetic component, but is mostly likely is due to a variety of environmental factors. First, young wolves, especially animals less than a year old, will weigh less than older adults of the same sex. The skeletons of adults do not grow after age 1, but they may continue to put on some muscle mass in the next year or two. Second, animals in packs that have had good hunting success and thus high food consumption will be fatter and weigh more than nearby pack members who haven't been so successful. This difference also is apparent for the same wolves in different winters when hunting is easier because snow is deep or because prey numbers have increased. Finally, adult wolf size is determined to some degree by nutrition as pups. Pups receiving less food in their rapid phase of growth in the summer will be smaller that well-fed pups, and this difference in skeletal and body mass size will remain apparent throughout their lives.

Color

Wolves are among the most variably colored mammal species, though some other canids also show striking variations. Arctic foxes can be either blue or white, sometimes depending on where their winter range is. Red foxes come in at least two colors as well: most are red, though with varying amounts of brown to yellowish gray mixed in, but some are black often with silver tips. African wild dogs have variable blotchy coloration of black, yellow and white. The variation is often so pronounced that individual dogs can be identified by human observers, based on the dog's distinctive coat color patterns. Also, wild dogs in the southern parts of Africa may have significantly more yellow in their coats than those in the more northern part of their range where they have more black.

Wolves, on the other hand, may have coat colors that range from white to cream-colored, tawny or reddish brown to steely gray, and salt-and-pepper to jet-black. Even a single individual may have white, black, brown, and gray hairs intermingled. In North America, less than 2% of wolves are white, but their proportion in the population increases going north from the taiga/boreal forest through the high Arctic of Canada and Greenland. There, more than 90% of wolves are white. White wolves remain white throughout their adult lives, but this is not necessarily true for other colors of wolves. In particular, repeated observations of known black wolves indicate that they sometimes change over their lifetimes to bluish-silver, silver, or even white. Gray colored wolves may also change to cream-colored or white over time. These changes in color may be due to advancing age, physiological stress, or inheritance of genes that tend to be expressed as white.

The proportion of black wolves in North America appears higher in the western and northwestern parts of the continent. Some packs may contain only black wolves, but others can have any proportion being black with most of the others some shade of gray; even wolf pups in the same litter may have differing coat colors. In south-central Canada and around the Great Lakes area most wolves are some shade of gray, and the occurrence of any black or white individuals in a pack is more notable. In Europe and Asia, coat color also varies, but gray or some shade of gray is most common, particularly in the southern, arid parts of its range.

Physical Adaptations

Coat

Not only is a wolf's coat colorful, but it is fully functional, as well. A wolf's coat is comprised not only of the stiff, long outer, or guard, hairs that give the wolf it's color, but also a shorter, finer layer of hair called the underfur. Many underfur hairs and one guard hair each arise from a single follicle, and the follicles themselves are often arranged in groups of three in a pattern all over the body. The purpose of the underfur is to provide insulation; that is, to trap air and create dead air spaces in which warm air and its heat is retained next to the skin. The guard hairs help cover the underfur and provide protection from rain or snow and from the wear of brush and other vegetation. Given this insulating purpose, it logically follows that wolves from more northerly latitudes and colder temperatures have much longer and denser fur than those from southern areas.

Skeleton

Canids, more so than any of the other carnivores, are adapted for traveling. And whether just exploring or hunting, wolves, along with African wild dogs, are widely known for their ability to trot or run for long periods of time. In fact, an old Russian proverb relates that a wolf is kept fed by its feet. It is not surprising, then, that wolves are "built" for travel. The large chest of a wolf is rather narrow, and its legs are positioned tight to the body with toes turned outwards. This allows a wolf to swing its legs easily and, in snow, to place its hind foot in the print made by the front foot (unlike dogs that put hind feet next to front foot prints). Another feature that allows wolves to do well in snow is their long, thin

Wolves vary in size across their geographic range, with those in India and Saudi Arabia weighing less than
half of those in northern Canada and Russia; in any one area, however, males usually weigh about 15% more than females.
Wolves also have highly variable coat colors, ranging from white to tawny to reddish-brown to gray to black.

legs. All canids walk on their toe tips, but wolves legs are relatively longer than their other close relations and thus are better able to get around in deeper snow. Also, a pack traveling through relatively deep snow usually follows one after the other; the tracks and trails made by other pack members reduces the energy needed to travel. However, wolves' relatively large feet also allow them to travel on top of crusted snow that may not support the narrow, sharp hooves of deer, moose, or elk. This allows them to move more quickly and thus be more efficient hunters.

Thin legs not only go through snow more easily than thick ones, but they also are easier to move and can thus be swung more quickly. Those that can be moved quickly allow for rapid and often long-distance, seemingly tireless movement. Wolves are both fast and enduring travelers. Walking wolves have been found to routinely travel at 6-10 km/hr (4-6 mi/hr), or twice the regular speed of a walking human. This allows wolves in the desert, for instance, to seek out necessary drinking water that might be available only at a few sites located at great distances from one another. Maximum speeds, as estimated from wolves chasing prey over short distances or, historically, humans in vehicles chasing wolves, likely reach 55-65 km/hr (35-40 mi/hr), again nearly twice the maximum speed of a human. Long-distance travels are also routine for wolves. A single, radio-tagged wolf followed by aircraft in Minnesota chased and followed a deer for at least 21 km (13 mi), and on Isle Royale, Michigan some packs have traveled an average of 50 km (31 mi) per day through snow in winter while hunting moose. On several occasions, biologists have documented wolf packs traveling 72 km (45 mi) in a 24-hour period. Although the total area over which a pack of wolves routinely travels varies in size depending on prey density and availability (see Chapter 5 – Land Use), a wolf pack in Alaska once ranged over an area of 12,000 km2 (5,000 mi^2) during 6 weeks of winter, and wolves dependent on migratory caribou in Canada may cover 100,000 km2 (40,000 mi^2) during the year.

Skull

Although a wolf's feet may help it get to prey that are bigger than they are, the process of killing and eating it would seem to be even more difficult. There are a variety of behavioral tactics for getting close enough to prey for a wolf to grab it with its teeth (see Chapter 8 – Food), but it is the wolf's skull and teeth, in particular, that are essential to capture and kill their prey. A wolf's skull is about 23-30 cm (9-12 in) long and a little more than half as wide. It tapers toward the front, forming the relatively long "nose" (compared to other carnivores) that is typical of canids. Importantly, the lower jaw is large and strong to provide space for teeth and attachment of massive jaw muscles. The jaw is well anchored to the skull because of the stress and strain it undergoes when helping to hold onto struggling prey, and is well-proportioned in length relative to skull width so that it can safely open quite wide.

Wolves possess 42 teeth as adults, including (from front to back) 12 incisors (6 on top and 6 on the bottom), 4 large canine teeth (1 each on top and bottom, and on each side), 16 premolars, and 10 molars. The largest and most notable of these are the canine teeth used to hold onto prey; they may measure 6.7cm (2.3 in) from tip to the base imbedded in the lower jaw. In cross section, wolf canine teeth are elliptical, suggesting that most of the stresses on these teeth are from front to back. This makes sense, as these teeth are used to stab, hold on to, and then pull at prey to try and drag it down. This grabbing action also serves to rip and cut hide and muscle, disabling and causing extensive bleeding of prey animals. In addition, prey pull at wolves, too, trying to get away or dislodge attacking wolves. One moose was seen dragging along a wolf, which had grabbed on to the moose's hind leg, for dozens of meters.

The small, front incisor teeth also help a wolf hold onto its prey, and often are needed when the largest of prey twist their heads back and forth and sometimes lift wolves off of the ground in

doing so. In addition, incisors are used to nip and pull at the skin and muscle of prey, too, thus combining with the canine teeth to make up a wolf's killing apparatus. These small teeth, however, are also used for more delicate tasks, including the capture of small mammals, removing bits of meat from bones, and picking of berries that also are included in a wolf's diet.

Once a prey animal is dead, a wolf's premolars and molars come into use. In particular, wolves (and in fact all carnivores) have a tooth configuration called the carnassials that are used specifically to slice through meat and hide. The upper fourth premolar and the lower first molar teeth are relatively enlarged and modified with shearing edges. When the jaws close, these blades shear past one another, trapping and cutting the food. These edges are also self-sharpening, thus providing life-long "meat scissors". Other premolars and molars are modified to serves as crushing and grinding surfaces. Though not as robust or pyramid-like as the teeth of bone-crushing hyenas, these teeth still allow wolves to crunch all but the largest and hardest pieces of prey.

Over the life of a wolf, all of their teeth become worn and somewhat rounded. Very old wolves may only have small nubs for incisors, and several may be missing. Sometimes canine teeth are broken off, and other teeth may become diseased and decayed. Still, as long as some of each remain, wolves usually continue to use them efficiently to process a wide variety of prey items.

Eyes, Ears, and Nose

The eyes of wolves are adapted to function both day and night, although their ability to both collect and exclude light is not nearly as good as that of cats. Wolves have a relatively wide view of their surrounding and do slightly better than dogs in using binocular vision to focus, but it is nowhere near the ability of humans. Dogs, and probably wolves, seem to be quite sensitive to motion and apparently see shades of gray better than do humans, but do have very poor color discrimination.

Dogs, and thus probably wolves, seem to have relatively ordinary hearing abilities for carnivores; but certainly can hear some things (e.g., howls) better than do humans (see Chapter 4 – Communication). Dog sensitivity to low frequencies is similar to that of humans and cats, though at higher pitches dogs become increasingly more sensitive than humans (and cats even more sensitive than dogs). The external ears, or pinnae, of wolves and dogs could serve to amplify a weak signal without moving the head; when facing some point of interest, wolves point their ears and seem alert. However, the ability of dogs (and wolves) to pinpoint the location of a sound is about 5 to 10 times poorer than that of humans, and the pinnae likely just help orient in general so that their eyes can take over.

Wolves use their noses for communication and for hunting. As such, it is a relatively strong sense due in large part to the long "nose" or rostrum that contains an estimated 280 million olfactory receptors, and to relatively large olfactory bulbs at the base of the brain. As a result, dogs, and presumably wolves, are 100's to millions of times more sensitive to odors than are humans. From what we know of dogs that sniff luggage at airports, or bloodhounds that track individuals through the woods, it seems reasonable that wolves are able to individually identify other wolves from their smells, as well as tell much about their social receptivity (see Chapter 4 – Communication). In addition, wolves likely find much of their prey at times via their noses. On Isle Royale, Michigan in the U.S., 43 of 51 hunts by a wolf pack for moose involved the wolves first detecting moose by scent from up to 300 m downwind; one cow with twin calves was scented from 2.4 km (1.5 miles) away.

Although a wolf's eyes and ears are key to survival, wolves are 100 times more sensitive to odors than humans.

Body

Once prey has been subdued, and food has been cut up or ground up to some extent by the teeth, other digestive processes take over. Although wolf saliva probably does not have any digestive enzymes in it (dog saliva doesn't), it still serves as a lubricant to help wolves swallow their food. Wolves eat rapidly and many of the pieces of meat are large chunks, sometimes as large as a caribou tongue or kidney (e.g., the size of a small pork chop). In addition to help drink water, slurp up blood, and lick meat off bones, a wolf's tongue is essential in swallowing whole such large pieces of prey.

The route to a wolf's stomach is a short esophagus where more mucous or lubricating fluid is added to food. Compared to the stomach of plant eating animals, that of a wolf is relatively simple because its diet consists mostly of highly concentrated and easily digestible fat and protein. It is also different from the stomach of a plant-eater because it has to have the capacity to hold a very large quantity of food – a wolf rarely can feed at leisure or at predictable intervals, so eating as much as possible as quickly as possible is essential. It has been reported that the stomach of a large dog can hold about 4 liters (1 gallon) of food. Similar values are not available for wolves, but maximum weight of food in a wolf's stomach has been measured several times. The stomachs of several dead wolves that had eaten poisoned bait in Canada weighed 5 kg (11 lbs), though they may have been able to eat even more if they had not died. One wolf killed in the wild in Russia had stomach contents weighing as much as 6 kg (13 lbs), but since the contents were mostly indigestible hair and bones, the investigator estimated that initially the meat that undoubtedly came with the hair and bones would have resulted in a total weight of perhaps 9 kg (20 lbs). Finally, ten captive 3-year-old wolves weighing an average of 41 kg (90 lbs) each were not fed for several days and then given all that they could eat; these wolves had stomach contents that weighed an average of 8 kg (18 lbs) each, or about 20% of the wolves' body weight.

Typically, the digesting mixture of meat, bone, hide, and hair continues through nearly 5.5 m (18 ft) of small intestine where much of the remaining nutrients are extracted and absorbed into the bloodstream. By the time the food remnants reach the large intestine, only wet gobs of hair, large chunks of hide, bone chunks, teeth, and other non-digestible materials remain. Water is usually absorbed from this mass before being excreted as relatively dry scats (feces or droppings). However, a wolf gorging on a freshly killed animal may at first consume only the highly digestible meat. In this case, non-digestible matter is minimal, and the resulting scats are dark and liquid. At one moose kill in Alberta, I found numerous "scats" on top of the snow that were really only dark liquid surrounding undigested meat chunks. The normal passage rate of food through a wolf is fast under any circumstances (usually only several hours), and in this case it was probably even faster to take advantage of the very large amount of food that was available to be eaten.

Again, the main reason that wolves have the ability to quickly swallow large chunks of food, store a very large portion of food in their stomach, and process it quickly only to eat more food is because of the "feast-or-famine" nature of wolf diets. Prey animals are usually very difficult to capture, and a single wolf has been known to go for several weeks in winter without making a kill. Thus, wolves have to eat all they can whenever they can. Wolves in packs usually kill a large ungulate every couple of days, but none are likely eat fresh meat every day. As a result, wolves typically lose and gain significant weight on a regular basis. A wolf that doesn't eat for 10 days may lose 8-9% of its body weight, but can gain weight back fairly rapidly by gorging on a fresh kill for several days. Wolves not able to make kills for many days, however, may starve to death after losing about a third of their body weight. This might occur where prey is scarce or very difficult to capture, and competition with pack mates or other carnivores is intense and the amount of meat that can be consumed at any kill is minimal.

Distribution:
Where do Wolves Live?

Historically

What does it say about wolves when we know that at one time, except for humans, they were the most widespread species of mammal on earth? They once roamed North America from central Mexico north to the Canadian Arctic, hunted in Europe from the tip of Italy to northernmost Norway, and denned in Asia from southern India to Japan and Siberia. Like several other canid species, wolves proved to be adaptable in many ways. They still lived amongst other large carnivores of various kinds, but were able to sustain themselves in a variety of ways and spread across more than half of the world.

It may be difficult to imagine that wolves once thrived on Manhattan Island, now the center of New York City, or trotted along the banks of the River Thames in London, England, or chased sika deer through birch forests that have been turned into the metropolis of Sapporo, Japan. But before humans developed agriculture and settled in villages 10,000-15,000 years ago, wolves occurred throughout the Northern Hemisphere.

The ability of wolves to live in all kinds of places is related to their diet and their tolerance of a variety of climatic conditions. Wolves can eat just about anything we humans can eat, plus a bit more that few of us find either nutritious or palatable. The major prey species of wolves (that is, the kinds of animals they get the most food from) are big mammals with hooves, called ungulates (see Chapter 8 – Food). They include all of the deer species like roe deer, white-tailed deer, caribou and reindeer, red deer and elk and moose, as well as bison and wisent, wild horses and asses, wild sheep and goats, wild boar, gazelles, musk oxen, and even camels. In other words, there is some kind of ungulate prey nearly everywhere and wolves, it turns out, can hunt any one of them successfully. Wolves may have to range far and wide to find vulnerable prey, and may even have to migrate with them throughout the year to make sure they have something to eat, but that's what wolves are good at.

Even where ungulate prey is very scarce or even absent, wolves are able to survive by eating other kinds of prey. In a few places in the North American Arctic, wolves feed mostly on Arctic hares that may weigh up to 5 kg (12 lbs). Also, wolves eat a lot of beavers or hares in some seasons, and even fill up on berries to help round out their diet. Wolves are notorious scavengers, as well. They will steal carcasses from other carnivores (e.g., bears) and eat the remains of prey they or other species killed days, weeks, or months (in the winter) previously. Overall, wolves eat such a varied array of food items that, given enough of whatever is available, wolves can survive almost anywhere.

In addition to their catholic taste in food, wolves have adapted physiological to widely varying environmental circumstances (see Chapter 2 – Morphology). Though wolves don't live in wet tropical rain forests, they do occur in many environments from hot deserts to temperate forests to Arctic tundra. In the foothills of Saudi Arabian mountains or the stony plains of the Gobi desert, wolves do just fine in summer temperatures of >40°C (>100°F), usually by sleeping during the day, like everything else, and hunting at night. In mid-winter above the Arctic Circle, when temperatures often reach <−40°C (−40°F) and the sun never gets above the horizon for weeks at a time, wolves curl up in the snow and have a good sleep when they are not chasing down musk oxen.

Wolves travel easily over flat plains or high mountain ranges, through desert sand, marshes, or lichen-covered tundra. They hunt

Except for humans, wolves were once the widest ranging mammal on earth, living in deserts, grasslands, forests, and Arctic tundra.

successfully in the thickest forests and the most featureless grasslands. They can swim great rivers, climb steep mountains, and can travel up to 50 km (30 mi) in a day. Given these abilities, it is not surprising that at one time we can easily imagine that wolves were seemingly everywhere.

That is not to say, however, that wolves were ever so numerous that one couldn't help but see one around every tree or grass clump. Wolf population density is determined by their food supply (see Chapter 7 – Populations) and except for migratory herds, even ungulates are not so dense as to see them readily. This is because it is an ecological certainty (because of energy loss in the ecosystem) that there is about 10–100 times more grass (in terms of weight or biomass) than there are animals that eat grass (herbivores, of which some ungulates are a fine example) and, similarly, 10–100 times more herbivore biomass than carnivore biomass. So, a pack of wolves, even where deer densities are very high, would still need a relatively large area (perhaps 50 km^2 [20 mi^2] at a minimum) to survive. At that density, one wouldn't run into a pack very often… Even so, one might speculate how many wolves lived in the world at any one time in the past. Given that there might be more than 120,000 wolves alive today (see below), and given the kinds and sizes of areas where wolves have been eliminated, it is not unreasonable to think that there may have been more than a million wolves once roaming the earth.

Currently

During the past 10,000 years, wolf distribution and numbers have been reduced, almost entirely the result of human activities, and mostly in the past 500 years (see Chapter 10 – Humans). Wolves and humans historically have competed for the same kinds of food (meat), and as a result there were likely always some wolves killed just as some bears or tigers might kill wolves. In addition, some wolves were killed to be eaten and for their

fur to serve as clothing. The biggest motivation for killing wolves was, however, for the protection of domestic livestock. As human populations spread, they took their livestock with them, and wolves were eliminated from areas where they were likely to prey on that livestock. The longer humans and their livestock remained in an area, the greater the chance that every last wolf in the area would be killed. Those areas inhabited by humans that were most isolated from larger populations of wolves that might recolonize an area, such as islands or peninsulas, were the first to have their wolf populations extirpated (completely eliminated). The British Isles, for example, have been without wolves for more than 400 years, many parts of Europe for several hundred years, and the large Island of Hokkaido, Japan for perhaps 150 years.

In the United States, most of the wolves were gone from the eastern half of the country 200 years ago, though some hung on until late in the 19th century. Even in the sparsely populated western half of the country (but an area settled primary for agriculture and livestock production), wolves were eliminated some 60 years ago. Wolves hung on along the southwestern border with Mexico until late in the 20th century, and in the western Great Lake states, and particularly the remote, unpopulated northeastern part of Minnesota, wolves never were completely eliminated.

At the turn of the 21st century, wolf populations in most areas were no longer declining as precipitously as in the previous century. In fact, many were increasing and expanding their range because of legal protection and purposeful reintroductions. In Europe, a population of 200–300 wolves in Portugal may be stable or declining slightly, but the 2,000 in Spain are stable. Italy's 450 wolves are expanding their range, and perhaps 40 have settled across the border in France. Germany has a few wolves that have immigrated from the population of about 700 in Poland to the east. There are perhaps 500 wolves in Croatia, Bosnia, and Herzegovina, a similar number in Slovakia, and as many as 2,500 in Romania. Sweden and Norway have only 80–95 wolves, and there are another 100 in neighboring Finland. In Estonia, Latvia, and Lithuania there are about 2,000, with more than 2,000 in Belarus and in the Ukraine. Bulgaria has 800–1,000, Greece 200-300, the Yugoslav Federation 500, Macedonia >1,000 and Macedonia and Albania >1,200. Turkey has perhaps 1,000 wolves, as well.

At the southern extent of their Eurasian range, wolves may number 300–600 in Saudi Arabia, and 1,000 in India. Lebanon, Israel, and Jordan may have >300 wolves, and Syria another 200. Unknown numbers, but perhaps 20,000–40,000, live in much of central Asia, and Russia may be home to as many as 30,000 wolves. There are perhaps 6,000–10,000 in China and reported to be as many 5,000–10,000 in Mongolia.

In North America, only a few wolves may live in Mexico, but 6,000–7,000 range over Alaska, and another 52,000 to 60,000 reside in Canada. In the Rocky Mountains of the United States, naturally recolonizing and purposefully reintroduced wolves now number more than 400, and in the Great Lakes States of Minnesota, Wisconsin, and the Upper Peninsula of Michigan there are more than 3,000 wolves. A reintroduction project for Mexican wolves in the southwestern U.S. has so far resulted in a

wild population of about 40.

As a species, the distribution and total number of wolves have been reduced substantially over the course of recent history. However, they are still thriving in much of the northern hemisphere; they number in the tens of thousands in each

A wolf family on Ellesmere Island in northern Canada.

hemisphere, and probably 140,000–180,000 in total. As long as there is food for wolves in the form of wild ungulates, and as long as people are able to tolerate and even value wolves, they will remain an important member of the Earth's fauna. Wolves are an adaptable species that has evolved a myriad of strategies and abilities to cope with their world.

Communication:
How do Wolves Communicate?

From personal experiences with dogs, and from what one might already know about wolves, one can guess that wolf senses must in some ways be highly tuned. Every dog that sniffs intently, and then lifts its leg on a bush or howls and barks at a passing siren gives us a good idea of the likely ways in which wolves communicate. Dog owners are attuned to the body and facial expressions of their own and other dogs.

Field biologists, trappers, hunters, and others have spent a lot of time trying to understand what wolves "say", sometimes by observing or hearing them directly, and other times by interpreting their "sign". Many of the more intimate details of wolf communication come from studies of captive wolves, dogs, and other closely related canids, but they certainly add valuable insights into the sensory world of wolves in the wild.

In scientific terms, communication involves one individual sending a specialized signal in a specific context, and one or more others receiving it. Signals are the behaviors and features of an animal that encode the information being transmitted. This information is intended to influence the recipient's expectations about what is about to happen next. Depending on the context, however, one animal's expectations might be different from another's, and as a result, a fight might occur when it really wasn't intended.

Communication signals used by a particular species vary considerably, but for any one type of signal there is some limit to its variability. This allows signals to be identified as discrete entities, but at the same time account for variation in both the sender's abilities and the information that the signal might contain. Also, some signals might also be combined in order pass along a different message.

Wolves do use signals that are obvious to us humans, but also use much more subtle but equally informative signals to send messages to other wolves. These signals span all the senses, and can either involve pack mates in close proximity, or neighboring and even unknown wolves from across the landscape (see below).

Auditory/Vocalizing and Hearing
Short-distance sounds

If you had the opportunity to listen at the entrance of a wolf den in springtime, chances are that you would hear a tiny cacophony of moans, squeals, and screams as pups wiggled around and searched for their mother's nipples. Although nearly anyone asked to name a wolf vocalization would indicate the howl, most wolf "calls" are relatively quiet and used at close range.

During the first 6 weeks of life, wolf pups seem to use at least 11 discrete vocal signals, and most of these have been produced at least once in the first 3 weeks. These include squeals, which are commonly ignored by the mother, and screams, which seem to be mild distress calls that often elicit grooming or repositioning by the mother. Pups also yelp, yawn, moan, whine, growl, bark, woof, squeak, and howl. Some of these sounds, such as moans that may be by-products of restful breathing, may serve only to reassure the mother that all is well. Others, such as growls and barks, are produced when pups are interacting with one another. Woofs likely reflect pup uncertainty, and squeaking is common as a response to adult squeaks and howls from outside the den. Howls are initially rarely produced, but once pups venture outside the den at the age of 3 weeks or so, they often join in with howling adults. They are usually more highly pitched and are not sustained for as long as are those of adults. About 15 percent of the time,

Wolf pups only six weeks old seem to use at least 11 different vocal signals, including squeals, yelps, whines, growls, and woofs.

pups vocalizations are mixed, probably indicating increasing levels of arousal or distress in pups.

Pups grow rapidly, and the common sounds of newborns begin to disappear as their ability to avoid or endure stressful situations increases. By the age of 3 weeks, when pups can see, hear, and move about easily, they begin to use sounds that are more adult-like. After another week or two, pups can actually produce all of the vocal signals used by adults, but it takes another 6 months or so for pups to grow into their voices and sound like adults.

Vocalizations of adults can generally be separated into two types, harmonic and noisy; both are used at short ranges where much of wolf vocalization takes place. Harmonic sounds include whines, whimpers, and yelps, and are used in friendly and submissive situations. These sounds are high-pitched and of purer tone, and end up sounding like they come from a relatively small animal; to signal friendliness, one should sound small rather than large. Such sounds are used in greeting and when trying to appease another wolf.

Noisy sounds, on the other hand, include growls, snarls, woofs, and barks that are used in aggressive and dominant contexts. These are sounds lower and coarser, and by their nature seem more aggressive. Wolves growl and snarl during a threat or attack, or as a warning. Growls are common when wolves are trying to assert their dominance. Woofs and barks are also used as warnings, and barks in particular can be used to draw attention to an animal.

Long-distance sounds

There is nothing quite like being woken up in the middle of night by a pack of howling wolves. It happened to me late one summer while I was camped out in the boreal forest of northern Alberta, investigating a wolf den used the previous spring. During the day, I collected scats from pups and adults to figure out later what they had been eating, and I mapped trails leading to and from the den. At night, after a quick dinner, the writing up of field notes, and some reading by flashlight, I fell asleep in my small tent, cozy in a sleeping bag. As far as I knew, there were no people within 30 km (18 miles) of where I lay. But sometime deep into the still night, the wolves started howling. I don't know if it was me just being there that set them off, or some other more canine motive, but I woke up quickly, stared at the ceiling of the tent, and just enjoyed the music.

When a wolf communicates vocally over a long distance, i.e., when they howl, wind turbulence, temperature, humidity, precipitation, noise, and the structure of the physical environment can all affect the sound that is made. Still, in forested habitats under ideal conditions such as a still, clear night, a wolf may hear other wolves howling as much as 10 km (6 miles) away, and in the open tundra, up to 16 km (10 miles) away. In comparison, some experiments that colleagues and I carried out with captive wolves in the forest suggest that we humans may only hear wolves up to 2 km (1.25 miles) away.

In order to minimize the distortion of the sound, howls are usually made at a lower frequency or pitch and are more harmonic than short-range sounds. These restrictions result in the more limited ability of howls to convey information, especially over the longest distances when they are at maximum volume. There is, however, noticeable variation in wolf howls, depending on the individual howler, the number of its companions, the distance between sender(s) and recipient(s), and the intent of the howl.

Howls of single, adult wolves may each last from 3 to 7 seconds, and bouts of such howling may last up to 9 minutes. In

Howls serve as the major long-distance mode of communication for wolves throughout the world.

captivity, single wolves howl most often during the winter breeding season and during morning and evening hours. Solo howls vary from sounding flat and evenly pitched to "breaking" howls that have pitch discontinuities. Their volume also seems to decrease and their "coarseness" seems to increase when approaching another howling wolf (or human). Finally, individual differences are noticeable to even the human ear. Some solo howls seem long, very low, and mournful, while others are higher pitched, variable, and almost stressed.

When wolves howl together, termed appropriately enough "chorus" howling, the result is even more variable than for solo howls. One or two wolves may begin with relatively plain howls, and then others rapidly join in with howls of higher pitches, varying patterns, and shorter lengths. In addition to howls, sometimes half of the concurrent sounds in a chorus howl are squeaks, barks, and growls. In general, chorus howls are characterized as mostly harmonious, with relatively little modulation, or as discordant. Pup choruses are often discordant, and choruses of adults are more harmonious. Also, choruses of howling adults seem more discordant when the wolves are in close proximity to one another, and more harmonious if each animal is separated from others by some distance. In general, any of these choruses usually last from 30 seconds to 2 minutes, and may be longer during the breeding season.

So, why do wolves howl? First of all, it seems clear that howling works to communicate both within and between packs. Although the evidence supporting various functions of howling ranges from speculative to quasi-experimental, at least four ideas seem reasonable. First, wolves may howl to reunite. Many observations have been made of separated wolves getting together after howling, and the likelihood that individual howls can be individually identified suggests that strangers can be told apart from pack mates. Also, howls by humans often result in nearby wolves quietly approaching the howlers. Second, wolves may howl to strengthen social bonds. Chorus howls seem to be highly contagious, except that wolves that have been expelled from a pack are otherwise being rejected to not join in howls. Also, there is vigorous social activity such as sniffing, and rubbing, and licking among pack mates before, during, and after chorus howls. Third, howling may serve to reinforce the spacing of wolves and wolf packs. Wolves responding to imitation howls generally hold their ground, while those that do not respond often move away. This is especially true at fresh kill sites where a carcass is an important resource to defend or, similarly, if wolves are accompanied by mobile pups. Although wolves do not seem to howl more often or forcefully at their territory boundaries, howling does seem to provide a mechanism where wolves can most easily avoid one another if they choose to do so. Finally, wolves may howl to find mates. Captive wolves often howl spontaneously during the breeding season. And although wild single wolves rarely howl back to single howls, they sometimes do approach the single howler, perhaps to cautiously find out if the howl was meant as a threat or an inducement. In sum, howling may have a variety of purposes, and no one who hears it will doubt that the wolves know what they're doing.

Olfactory / Smelling

If a human could be a wolf for a day, it is likely that the biggest difference in life would concerns odors. The olfactory world of a wolf is so much more rich and varied and hidden than what we humans can perceive, that perhaps only our own communication through language rivals the scent messages of wolves.

Sources

As one might suspect, it is not so easy to identify the sources of a myriad of odors and scents when we, ourselves, are so olfactorily inept. However, from histological studies of wolf and dog tissue, coupled with behavioral observations and careful collection of various canine excretions, we do have some idea of how wolf smells are produced.

There are 3 basic kinds of wolf skin glands that seem to produce substances that, when acted upon by various bacteria, produce distinct odors. Sebaceous glands usually associated with hair follicles produce an oily, waxy substance called sebum; apocrine sweat glands produce watery secretions from the face, lip, back, and between the toes; and eccrine glands, the true sweat glands that provide for cooling, secrete a salty fluid only on the foot pads. The activity of these skin glands varies seasonally with changes in hormone levels. In addition, the paired sacs just inside a wolf's anus also contain apocrine and sebaceous glands and are surrounded by muscle that is under voluntary control. Thus, wolves can deposit secretions from these anal sacs at will.

Secretions reflecting sexual odors are produced by preputial glands in the penis and vulva, and by the vagina and uterus. Much of the sniffing and licking of genital areas by wolves of both sexes likely reflects these specific odor-producing glands. Wolves often lick each other's muzzles, and this may be a result of sebaceous glands on the lips, or possibly saliva, which contains high concentrations of hormones. Finally, the most studied means of canid olfactory communication is urine-marking; perhaps this is because it is so common and obvious to dog owners and followers of canid trails in the snow. The chemical composition of urine, as an excretory product, certainly varies with diet. However, it also likely varies in hormone content throughout the year (breeding vs. non-breeding seasons), and in content and composition of prepucial and vaginal secretions that wash into the urine. Urine is individually identifiable by wolves, as well.

Messages

Wolf olfactory messages likely contain information on species, individual identity, age, gender, social rank, and reproductive status. The apocrine glands in the webs between the toes and the eccrine glands on the toe pads likely come into use when wolves do stiff-legged scratching of the ground that sometimes follows urine-marking and defecation by breeding wolves. These are probably recognition signals to any wolf that happens by the urine or scat deposition site. Sebaceous and apocrine glands at the base of hair follicles on a wolf's shoulders may exude their contents when the wolf raises it's the hair on its neck and back. The odors

Wolves constantly monitor odors in their environment.

might help signal the state of arousal and or aggression/fear of the signal sender. Sebaceous and apocrine glands on the top surface of the tail about a third of the way from its base probably excrete passively, such as when it gets rubbed onto the roof of a den entrance. These would seem to be recognition signals, as well. When wolves meet each other and mutually sniff near the anus, scents from anal sacs likely aid in recognition. These glands also seem to be used in reproductive communication; only during the breeding season do female wolves usually investigate another wolf's anal area. Finally, wolves may expel anal sac secretions when they are highly stressed. Because secretions from anal sacs are

often deposited on scats during defecation, these communication signals are not only used during direct interactions with other wolves, but are also used for communication long after the depositor has moved on. When compounds isolated from vaginal glands of estrous ("in heat") females have been later applied to spayed females, they have elicited arousal and mounting attempts by males. Saliva concentrations of hormones may contain information on gender and reproductive state, as well.

Finally, it seems that urine-marking, in both male and female wolves is importantly related not only to spacing of individuals or family groups, but also to reproduction, advertising proestrus and estrus, establishing a pair bond, and even to catalog food. Wolves urine-mark more frequently along the boundaries of their territories than in the interior, creating an "olfactory bowl" and letting other wolves know of their presence. Many of these marks occur in prominent places, both high on an object (i.e., at nose level, the result of a "raised-leg" urination), and on a noticeable object.

In both wolves, males urine-mark more than females, and both males and females, particularly dominant ones, urine-mark more during the breeding season. Often during the breeding season, urine-marks of paired males and females are deposited on top of one another and this behavior is likely related to formation and maintenance of the pair bond. Finally, wolves are known to urine-mark food caches that have been emptied, thus keeping track of the status of stored food and making more efficient use of their foraging time.

One remarkable aspect of scent-marking is that it is done so frequently. Products of urine-marking, defecation, and ground scratching are left, on average, about every 240 m (800 ft) throughout wolf territories, especially along regular routes and at trail or road junctions. The fact that these marks are made so

regularly attests to their efficiency at communicating their intent.

The Scent-rolling Enigma

Wolves have a habit, the same one as is universally considered disgusting in dogs, of rolling in the scent of pungent, sometimes putrid, substances. These substances may include rotted carcasses, feces, or other gag-inducing scents. This is a very ritualized behavior and seems to bring great joy to the canids that engage in it. Although tests with captive wolves have generated long lists of scent-rolling stimuli, the only guesses of its function include the familiarization with novel odors, some strong attraction or aversion to particular odors, concealing one's own scent with an alternative, or increasing attractiveness by applying a novel odor. The last suggestion is supported by the observation that female African wild dogs rubbed in the urine of males whose pack they were attempting to join.

Visual / Seeing

Postures and expressions are perhaps the easiest of wolf communication modes for we humans to recognize, again because of our close relationship to dogs. A crouching wolf with tucked tail seems to tell us something very different than one with bared teeth and raised hair along the neck and back, or another with upright head, a wide grin and a wagging tail. Just as we interpret human gestures and facial cues as important forms of communication, so do wolves.

Visual communication, however, has sometimes been difficult to characterize quantitatively. It is not as obvious as vocal communication; visual signals come and go more subtly and may be combined with a number of other visual signals simultaneously. Still, by describing what wolves do under various circumstances many times over, we have identified patterns that give us good

Wolves urine-mark often when travelling for a variety of reasons, including advertising their presence and reproductive status.

insight for what kinds of information wolves are transmitting and receiving visually.

Visual wolf communication is carried out via the face, the body, and the tail. Signals from ears, eyes, lips, teeth, nose, forehead, changes in body posture, and erectile hair can be enhanced by coloration of the face and body. These signals are useful when wolves are in close proximity to one another because they can be quickly and easily interpreted, avoiding unnecessary misunderstanding or confrontation.

In general, these signals reflect one continuum of expression from submissive to dominant and another, simultaneously, from playful to serious. For example, when a single, dominant wolf returns to a den from a hunt, any other wolf will likely run to greet it. This greeting wolf might approach in a low posture with a slightly crouched body, ears back and close to its head, and a wagging tail. It will likely nuzzle and lick the mouth and face of the returning wolf that, in return, stands erect with head up and tail flying high. The somewhat playful but actively submissive greeter exchanges information with the dominant, somewhat serious returnee. Similarly, confrontational interactions between two wolves often lead to one wolf on its side and back, tail curled between its legs and ears flat and directed backwards, and the other wolf standing over it with teeth bared, hair raised, and ears erect. The passively submissive wolf and the actively dominant wolf are both quite serious, and social order is maintained.

Active and passive submission in adult wolves reflects behaviors used as pups (food begging and response to licking – see below) but transformed into related behaviors as adults. Similarly, dominance behavior developed in play-fighting among pups carries over into adult interactions that reduce pack conflict. These behaviors are expanded and combined to transmit complex information on mood, intention, and current status. They are often combined, as well, with auditory and/or olfactory signals to make the intended messages even clearer.

Tactile / Touching

Tactile communication in newborn, blind pups is evident in their efforts to nurse and huddle together to keep warm. In their early weeks, pups are stimulated to urinate and defecate by their mothers licking of their groin area. As they get older, much of their play involves frequent body contact, and much of their food-begging behavior involves licking and other direct contact with food-providing adults.

For adults, much of their body contact occurs in friendly situations such as group greetings and ceremonies, and during courtship and play. Other tactile communication may occur during aggressive encounters. When pushing and shoving, and even bites, certainly send strong signals of intent or desire.

Tactile communication may reduce stress and strengthen social bonds. This anxiety reducing behavior has been shown with studies of humans and their pet dogs, and certainly wolf pups seem reassured when physically comforted by their pack mates. In addition, physical contact during aggressive encounters likely helps wolves assess each other's physical strength and skill.

Gustatory / Tasting

We don't really know much at all about the gustatory abilities of wolves, nor how tastes might help in communication. Certainly it is adaptive for a wolf to be able to tell sweet, ripe berries from unripe ones. But the taste of a freshly killed moose vs. one that has been rotting in the sun for days does not seem to affect consumption rates of the meat. There is the possibility that chemical information in urine or glandular secretions can be tasted and interpreted, but there have been no studies of such abilities. Although there is no good reason to believe that a wolf cannot detect salty, bitter, sweet, or sour substances (dogs possess the same kinds receptors as humans with regard to these categories of taste), their preferences and abilities with regard to taste will likely remain a mystery for some time to come.

Land Use:
How do Wolves use Their Environment?

Wolves live in a wide variety of landscapes, and one might expect their use of these different kinds of places to vary as widely. The density and distribution of wolves, however, is determined by a relatively few factors (for example, see Chapter 7 – Wolf Populations), and so there is a consistency to the way in which wolf movements and activities are adapted to the land. Whether in India or Poland, Mongolia or Alaska, wolves need to move around to find things to eat, to find mates, and to find sites where their pups can be born and raised; they also need to avoid getting in harm's way.

Home Ranges and Territories

A home range is the area over which an animal travels in the course of finding food, mates, rest, and sanctuary from predation. Some individual animals are truly nomadic for at least part of their lives; that is, they travel in seemingly random directions and patterns. But most animals end up returning to the same places over and over again and have what we describe as home ranges. We also presume that this strategy of constantly familiarizing themselves with a particular area must have important survival benefits.

If animals have to compete with others of their kind for resources, and if it is both feasible and economical to do so, some species actively defend the integrity of their home range; a defended home range is called a territory. Generally, wolves are considered to be highly territorial. They make special efforts to advertise their presence on a piece of land to other wolves and they sometime will fight to the death to defend it. Defending territories is a very adaptive behavior for wolves because they need only "win" once or twice in actual confrontations to maintain

their claim. Subsequently, they expend much less energy and avoid much more risk by just leaving "signposts" such as scent marks, mostly near the perimeter of their territory, to keep other wolves out. This leaves them much needed time for hunting, mating, and caring for pups.

Under normal circumstances, many wolf territories are inherited. Because some pups and older animals stay with the pack throughout their lives, the territories they live in are essentially passed on to them when their parents die. In several places where wolves have been studied for long periods of time, generations of wolves have remained fairly sedentary and their territories don't really change much from year to year, or even decade to decade. Many other potential wolf territories are "discovered" by dispersing wolves (see below). These wolves have left their packs to find mates and territories on their own. Either alone, or sometimes with a newfound mate, they may come across vacant areas that seem to have the necessary resources for survival. These areas may have once been used by wolves, even by a territorial pack, but are vacant because the pack recently disappeared. The wandering pair of wolves also may discover some "new" area that has not had wolves for a very long time. Finally, some wolves acquire a territory by taking over part or all of the territory of another pack of wolves. It may be that some mortality factor has reduced the pack to a size that is insufficient to defend their territory. Often, a single wolf or two will have died, but socially there is an "opening" for a wolf, and a disperser may end up joining a pack.

The location of wolf territories is often tied directly to prey type and behavior. This is because food is the major resource for wolves, and because wolf food in the form of ungulates and other

Wolf packs range wide and far, usually throughout home ranges that are defended from other packs.

prey is usually hard to find and hard to catch. First of all, most species of prey have specific habitat preferences themselves, and thus are found more often in certain types of places than in others. When wolves figure out the distribution of their prey, their movements and thus the location of their territories reflect the choices of the prey. Second, some species are solitary (moose, for example), some are gregarious (musk ox), and some switch between these grouping behaviors, depending on the season (red deer that are grouped in harems with a dominant male during the breeding season, or white-tailed deer that congregate in the winter in places where the snow is not so deep). These behaviors are reflected in the overall distribution of prey; that is, whether prey are clumped or spread out. Again, wolf movements will reflect this distribution. Finally, the movements of the individual prey animals themselves will affect the degree of territoriality of wolves. Prey that have small home ranges themselves will seem relatively sedentary to wolves, and a wolf pack's territory might consistently contain the amount of prey required for wolves to persist. However, some prey animals move over relatively large or very large areas during the course of the year. In these circumstances, territorial behavior might not be as assertive as when prey are relatively sedentary, and wolves will not defend their ranges in the same way. For example, caribou in the American Arctic may move thousands of kilometers (throughout areas of >60,000 km^2 [25,000 mi^2]) during annual migrations; central Asian saiga antelope may migrate over similar distances and areas. For wolves that depend only on these caribou for food, the best survival strategy is to move with the caribou when they can, and when they can't (during the denning season) they make many long trips to hunt caribou. It is clear that for a large part of the year, territorial behavior is not employed because neither wolves nor prey are in any one spot long enough to make it worthwhile. On the other hand, the seasonal movement of prey such as mountain sheep might be shorter (essentially up and down local mountains), and these sheep may have fairly localized seasonal ranges. Under these circumstances, wolves may remain territorial, but their territorial boundaries may shift seasonally to reflect the distribution of their prey. Finally, some, but not all, white-tailed deer may migrate a fair distance away from a wolf pack's territory during winter. In this case, wolves might remain on and defend their annual territory but in winter may make trips out to deer concentrations that are in no pack's territory.

The size of wolf pack territories varies by orders of magnitude across their geographic range; some have been measured that are as small as 33 km^2 (13 mi^2) and others are as large as 4,335 km^2 (1,674 mi^2). Of course this does not include the home ranges of non-territorial wolves that follow migratory prey, such a wolf monitored in Canada that, in the course of a year, traveled over an area of >100,000 km^2 (>40,000 mi^2). The ultimate cause of this great variation in territory size is, not surprisingly, the type and abundance of prey. Where moose are the primary prey of wolves, territory size is inversely correlated with moose density; that is, where moose are more common, territories are smaller. The same thing has been shown for wolves living in areas where white-tailed deer are the primary prey. In a more general sense, this relationship holds throughout the entire distribution of wolves. Wolf territories are generally smaller at lower latitudes, and larger at higher latitudes. This pattern corresponds to higher productivity at lower latitudes, and relatively higher prey densities. So, in general, wolf territories are smaller where prey density and biomass is higher.

One might suspect that wolf territory size also varies with pack size; the larger the pack, the bigger the territory, because more wolves need more food. In reality, this is only sometimes true. It turns out that when a pair of wolves first establishes a territory, they stake out an area much bigger than needed for just two wolves. In essence, they anticipate the production of 4-6 pups, and an ultimate pack size much larger than in the beginning. Territory sizes seem to reflect not just the number of wolves in a pack at any given time, but some anticipated or average pack size. As a result, territory sizes in a given area do not differ that much among packs. Some large packs of 15 adult-sized animals certainly have, over time and given equivalent prey densities, larger territories than pack one-third their size. But over the course of a year or two, as the number of wolves in a pack changes, territory boundaries may shift as needed territory size grows or diminishes. And in the long run one cannot easily predict territory size just from the number of wolves one might count in a pack.

Theoretically, a maximum number of wolf territories could be packed on to a landscape if every one of them was the same size and they were placed in a honeycomb pattern of hexagons. Wolf territories are not arranged as perfect hexagons, but when mapped with the boundaries scientists and naturalists are able to identify, they do appear as a tightly packed mosaic, usually with very little space between them. Of course, landscape features often dictate the size and shape of boundaries. Lakes and rivers often form natural territory edges because they represent areas not easily traversed, and are easily recognized. Marshes and swamps may also form boundaries for much the same reason. Large areas with few or no prey animals may also separate territories; one can easily imagine this for desert areas on the edge of territories, but in Alberta a large expanse of dense jack pine forest seemed to have the same effect.

The actual shape of territories is affected not only by landscape features, but also by the logistics of defending the boundary via scent marking or howling. Geometrically, a circle has the smallest edge-to-area ratio; that is, the perimeter of a circle is shorter for a circle of given area than it is for any other shape. The more a territory shape deviates from a circle, the longer the perimeter in relation to its area. A short perimeter means less effort scent marking, and a circle means a shorter distance to any edge and thus more efficient vocal communication. As a result, most wolf

territories look more like hexagons than long, narrow polygons. An example of this efficiency is found on Isle Royale, the large island in Lake Superior in North America where 10-50 wolves have lived for the past 50 years. The 544-km^2 (210-mi^2) island is about 5 times as long as it is wide. When 2 or 3 packs are present, their territories almost always cover the width of the

Territories are defended to ensure pup survival.

island, and are thus rounder than they are long and skinny. This way packs can take advantage of having lots of shoreline in their territory that doesn't need marking, and only a small (island-wide) strip of boundary that actually needs to be defended.

It is easy to think of wolf territory boundaries as static fences that rarely have to be moved, and some topographic features may make this true. But in general, these boundaries are not static and change constantly, sometimes in small ways and sometimes in large. First of all, because boundaries are most often demarcated by wolf urine or scats deposited at intervals of 10s and 100s of meters over periods of days and weeks, and maintained with extremely infrequent confrontation, they are not so much fences as they are buffer zones which may be 1 to >5 km (0.6-2 mi) wide. If wolves are in some ways able to communicate and detect size of adjacent packs, a large aggressive pack may feel more comfortable pushing their boundary outward into the territory of a smaller pack (see Chapter 6 – Social Behavior). Even small changes in territory boundaries may mean large changes in territory size. For example, a territory of 150 km^2 (58 mi^2) has a radius of about 7 km (4.3 mi). If pack members were able to extend the boundary an additional 1 km (0.6 mi) in every direction, the territory would encompass 200 km^2 (77 mi^2), an increase of 33%.

Changes also occur seasonally. Territory sizes measured by scientists in the summer often are smaller than in the winter. This makes sense given that prey density increases significantly because of reproduction, and thus wolves likely find hunting easier. Seasonal shifts in boundaries may also occur when prey distribution shifts significantly, but not so much that territoriality is abandoned.

The most noticeable shifts in territory boundaries occur when wolf populations change dramatically, paticularly when they increase. For colonizing or recolonizing populations, adjacent wolf packs may be few or none, and thus little or no competition that might require actively maintained territory boundaries. During the course of colonization, pack boundaries can change dramatically and territories themselves have even shifted 50 km as new wolves move into an area or are added to the population. As wolf populations become saturated, and more and more territories fill up an area, the opportunity to dramatically change boundaries without much consequence is greatly reduced, and some semblance of boundary stability thus takes over. Territory boundaries change relatively less often when populations are declining. If only a few resident wolves in a pack remain, they still maintain their original territory in anticipation of increasing the pack size the next year (much like newly established packs described above). If entire packs are eliminated, adjacent packs might take over the vacant territory, but not if they are too slow and a new pair of wolves moves in.

Dens and Home Sites

Dens are the places where wolf pups are born. They usually are located away (>1 km; 0.6 mi) from the edges of a pack's territory because these are places where conflicts with other wolf packs would be more common, and thus more perilous places to raise pups. Within the core of small territories, den sites seem rather randomly placed, though in large territories without many physical features such as rivers, mountains, or roads, dens are noticeably more centrally located.

The choice of a den site may be influenced by experience, but obviously wolves breeding for the first time in an area unfamiliar to them must pick out a location with the help of some innate sense of what will suffice. One prerequisite seems to be relatively close proximity to open water. Because a den must provide protection for the pups, both from rain, snow, and flooding, and from predators, it is usually a covered tunnel and hole of some type.

Wolves often dig these dens themselves, and some may even be dug months ahead of time. These earthen dens are usually dug in relatively sandy, well-drained soils, often into hillsides. It is important that the roof of the tunnel and den are structurally supported to avoid collapse. As a result, tunnels in the forest are dug under well-rooted trees, those on sandy bluffs in the Arctic are dug under a think root-mat of vegetation, and in a variety of situations are dug into relatively steep hillsides. Where the roof is not well supported and tunnels sometimes collapse, multiple entrances to dens are common.

Many wolf dens are not dug by the wolves themselves. For instance, they may enlarge burrows previously dug by foxes or

The raising of pups is a major focus of spring and summer activities for a wolf pack. Birth sites may be in earthen dens, rock caves, hollow logs, and even abandoned beaver lodges. Subsequent home sites, or nursery areas, may be near food sources that the pups can exploit. All pack members contribute to pup rearing.

Dens and pup nursery areas serve as the centers of wolf pack activity, but individual wolves travel widely to hunt and then bring food back to the pups and other attendant adults. Large food items may be carried in the mouth, but chunks of meat are brought home in the stomach and then regurgitated.

other animals. Use of rock caves is common, and one in the Canadian Arctic presumably has been used off and on by wolves as a den for the past 700 years. In Alberta, Canada I found wolves denning in an abandoned beaver lodge, and in Minnesota one female raised a litter of pups in a large hollow log that remained from logging that occurred perhaps 70 years previously.

Tunnels to wolf dens are usually a bit wider than they are high, and a human adult can fairly easily crawl into a den. Often the tunnel slopes downward at a slight angle. The tunnel may lead straight to a den chamber or may have a distinct bend. Some are only 1-2 m (3-7 ft) long, but some may reach more than 4 m (13 ft). Chambers in dug dens are large enough for a female to turn around in, and to comfortably but snugly accommodate herself and a litter of nursing pups. Thus, they are noticeably taller than the tunnel, but still wider in all dimensions than they are high.

Wolf pups live in and around dens for the first 8 weeks of their lives. Sometimes on their own, and sometimes as a result of disturbance, female wolves may move their pups to a second or even third den during this time. By the time pups are 8 weeks old, however, they spend most of their time above ground, and they are able to walk well enough to be moved more easily and safely than when they were younger. Thus, during the next 12 weeks of their lives they are moved to different places within the pack's territory that are not considered dens, but are referred to as "rendezvous" or "loafing" sites. One can think of these areas as wolf nursery areas where the pups stay put but the older animals in the pack all return to after foraging trips. Often these sites are near or at food sources that the pups can exploit. Several I have visited were in the middle of blueberry or raspberry patches, and others were at the carcasses of a moose or deer that the pack had either killed or discovered dead. Upon approaching one of these rendezvous sites, the abundance of wolf trails increases and most lead directly to some relatively open area with grass packed down and a myriad of small trails that the pups have used. Wolf scats

abound and it is easy to imagine the play that goes on while adults mill about or are gone hunting.

Movements within Territories

When pups are born, the den site serves as the center of pack activity. This is because pups, as the packs most valuable resource,

Wolves may be away from pups for several days.

require constant attention and all pack members feed pups. Thus, older wolves rest at or near the den site, and then leave in all directions to hunt by themselves or with others, returning after hours or days to bring food back to weaned pups. Sometimes pack members will leave for extended periods of time, but they always return to the den to make contact with pack mates. This pattern of movement continues throughout the time that pups are at to rendezvous sites, and thus until pups are 20 weeks of age.

After 20 weeks of age, wolf pups have grown large enough to travel with the other adults in the pack. The two main functions that travel fulfills are foraging (hunting and scavenging) and territory maintenance (learning the boundaries). When these two functions can be fulfilled simultaneously, and they usually are, so much the better.

Most often, wolves follow trails, shores, gravel bars, frozen waterways, ridges, and roads. More particularly, they most often follow the trails of other animals, even if seemingly easy paths across bare ground or a frozen lake are available. They usually follow each other single file, especially through deep snow to make travel easier, though they often spread out a bit on bare terrain. Movements within the pack's territory are seemingly nomadic, though they often pass by places where they have spent times as pups. Rest sites are most often associated with places where the pack has made kills. Resting wolves will take advantage of dry spots, or those free of snow in the bright sunshine, unless none are available. Then they just curl up wherever they can and wait until the next hunt begins. In some places such as central Italy, however, where wolves co-exist with extensive human populations, and thus more permanent food resources such as garbage dumps, they usually don't roam throughout their territory during most of the year. Rather, they continue to rest in one area and forage each night from that location.

In many places wolves travel the same routes, likely because they are easy to traverse, lead to and go through areas where prey is more concentrated, and/or are at the boundaries of territories. Actual circuits of travel described for wolves are more common in mountainous terrain where ease of travel is a more important matter than in flat homogeneous terrain.

Extraterritorial Movements

There are many reasons why wolves occasionally travel outside of their territory. This first is to find a mate and locate a territory in which to settle and raise a family. This process of leaving one's natal pack is called dispersal (see Chapter 6 – Social Behavior). The way in which wolves travel outside of their territory is apparently not much different to that of inside their territory, except that they often move away from their natal territory. They still follow trails and ridges, look for and spend time in areas with higher prey densities, and, importantly, respect the territorial marking of other wolves. Again, this response to scents, scratches, and howls is similar to what it would be within the home territory, except that there is no safe place to retreat. Thus, the movements of dispersing wolves seem a little more erratic as they "bounce" off the boundaries of established territories while making their way across the landscape. Sometimes wolves do not travel often or far to seek out a mate and a place to reproduce. One yearling male wolf in central Minnesota dispersed, and in the next few days traveled several miles into the adjacent pack's territory, found out that the dominant male of the pack was missing (recently dead), bonded with the adult female, and settled down. In other circumstances, wolves may disperse several times in a winter, making long treks over huge areas, unable to find a mate or potential territory and returning home without success. Some wolves also disperse and just keep traveling away from their natal range, ending up 200-550 km (125-350 mi) from the next nearest wolves before settling down or, more likely, being killed by any number of things (see Chapter 7 – Populations).

Another reason wolves leave their territory is to find food. This is especially dangerous when these travels lead not just along trails of migratory prey, but into the territories of other wolves. These "trespasses" are especially common when prey is hard to find or capture, and wolves are therefore desperately hungry. One gets the sense that they are either sneaking into an adjacent territory, hoping that the residents happen to be on the far side of the range, or are confident enough in their abilities to confront other wolves, that they just go and get what they need. In almost all cases, the wolves return to their own territory relatively quickly. If not, they are usually confronted by the resident pack, and this can lead to deadly combat (see Chapter 7 – Populations).

Social Behavior:
How do Wolves Interact with Other Wolves?

One of the things that most influences people's fascination with wolves is their social behavior. We know that they live in families, with both parents and sometimes older brothers and sisters helping to take care of pups. We have the classic image of a string of wolves traveling through the snow in search of prey; we also know that when they find prey, they will work collaboratively in the dangerous job of bringing it down. Wolves play intensively with each other, but they also sometimes fight and even kill one another. Humans relate to wolves as social beings because they seem to show a variety of social behaviors similar to our own.

Finding Mates

As mentioned in Chapter 5 – Land Use, a portion of any wolf population is comprised of single wolves that have left their packs (i.e., dispersed) in search of a mate and a territory. They may travel for days or weeks throughout both immediately adjacent areas and unknown areas farther from home. They are aware of scent marks made by territorial wolves, but also search for signs of single wolves of the opposite sex. When such a sign is found, wolves probably trail each other warily, emit appropriate vocalizations, come within sight of a potential mate, and make the appropriate physical gestures indicating non-aggressive attitudes. Some intensive olfactory investigations are undertaken, a bit of playful interactions occur, and if personalities match, a pair is formed. These behaviors may occur right at the edge of a "natal", or home territory (the establishment of a new territory in such a location has been termed "budding"), or several hundred miles away.

Initial searches for mates are sometimes focused on finding single wolves, but other times a breeder is needed in an established pack. This happens when male or female dispersers find, meet up with, and are adopted by another family; a bond is formed with the mateless wolf and the pair is formed.

Another means of pair formation is the taking over of a breeding position by a wolf that is already a member of the pack. Most often, such pack members are adoptees; that is, dispersers from other packs that have become members of a different pack, but not initially in the role of a breeder. Sometimes, however, wolves born into a pack that are of breeding age don't leave. One may stay in the pack, like the adoptees identified above, and bide their time until an older breeder of the same sex steps aside, leaves, or dies. They then step into the role of breeder.

To complicate our understanding of wolf families even more, there are circumstances when more than one female in a pack breeds. Usually this occurs when food supplies are high, either the result of an ungulate population increase or the heavy mortality of wolves due to disease or harvesting (and thus a relative increase in food availability). In these cases, it is not entirely clear if just one male mates with both females, or if two males are involved. It had been previously thought that inbreeding might be common in these circumstances, and that a male wolf would breed with his mate and their daughter. More recent genetic evidence suggests that either two males are involved, the second likely an adoptee wolf from another pack, or that the one wolf that does the breeding is an adoptee and thus unrelated to either of the females.

Finally, it is under the conditions of multiple breeding pairs of wolves occurring in a single pack that pack splitting occurs. This usually happens when pack sizes get quite large (12-20), and each pair leaves with about half of the pack members. Each new pack

Wolves interact constantly, most often with pack mates but also on occasion with wolves outside of their family.

takes over a portion of the original range, and appears to continue with wolf family life as a pack with a single pair of breeders. When the two packs meet, they sometimes greet each other as family, but then usually go their separate ways.

Courtship and Breeding

The seasonal peak in courtship behavior and mating correlates with changes in levels of reproductive hormones. In the fall, testosterone levels begin rising in males, as do estrogen levels in females. When wolves have mates, or as soon as they find one, they begin to show more interest in them, even if such interest is not returned. Males seem to be a bit more aggressive, as well. For the two months prior to actual breeding, paired wolves sleep closer to one another than at other times of the year. Also, the breeding female in each pack is followed more closely by her mate than by other pack members. The paired wolves nuzzle each other, prance, and investigate each other's genitals more often, and when traveling they seem to scent-mark more often.

In February when the female is actually in estrus (ready to mate), the pair may show keen interest in one another by pawing and rubbing against each other. The estrus period usually lasts about a week, perhaps two, and that is the only time of the year that she can become pregnant. When the wolves finally decide to mate they do so in the same way as dogs. This includes the "copulatory tie" when the male and female cannot separate for 5-30 minutes; after the male dismounts the pair usually rests by standing or lying rear to rear. The total number of times a pair may copulate varies, and has averaged about 5 or 6 times for captive wolves.

The breeding of wolves is timed such that pups are born early enough in spring, usually early to late April, to take advantage of the birth pulse of herbivores. A new and plentiful supply of prey means that pups have a better chance of growing fast before the next winter. Since gestation of pups within a pregnant female takes 61 to 64 days, breeding must occur in early to late February.

This means that pairs must have come together at least by then, and assuming some courtship activity, probably earlier. In fact, new pairs of wolves can form at all times of year, and existing pairs remain together year round.

Why do Wolves Live in Packs?

What is it about living in a pack that makes it worthwhile for almost all wolves to do so, or at least to want to do so? For one thing, there is great variation in the rate at which wolves mature. Though most seem capable of breeding at age 2, some are not ready at age 3, and physiologically wolves may not be fully mature until age 5. Thus it behooves immature wolves to stay with parents until they are fully developed. This way, they can continue to be nurtured by their parents, as well as continue to learn the finer points of finding and capturing adequate prey. From the parent's point of view, continued investment in immature offspring better ensures that their reproductive efforts will pay off in the future (i.e., their pups will have pups).

In addition, food seems to be an important factor in determining wolf group size. It has often been suggested that wolves living in packs are more efficient than individuals at capturing relatively big prey, the kind that wolves typically rely on. This is probably true, up to a point. For example, small packs studied in Italy and Israel tended to feed mostly on garbage and small animals, while large packs in Canada and Alaska fed on moose and bison. Still, single wolves have been known to kill, without assistance, even the largest of prey, e.g., adult moose, musk oxen, and bison. In addition, studies of pack size and per capita consumption (i.e., the amount of meat that each wolf gets over time) indicate that very large packs are less efficient killers than are packs even half their size. So, why do wolves live in packs? The best explanation is that several wolves are, indeed, more efficient at finding and killing large prey than a single wolf or even a pair of wolves. The fact that wolves take the chance of killing large prey at all is likely because such prey can, even though they are irregularly distributed at relatively low density, provide so much food for the effort expended. It is the characteristics of the prey (high food quantity, patchy distribution) that make pack living a worthwhile endeavor. Importantly, the reason that pack sizes occasionally get much larger than is most efficient (only a few pack members are really required to kill the prey), is simply because they can. That is, because there is so much food available once the prey is killed, more wolves than needed to kill the prey can feed on it. This suits packs with high reproductive rates, because they can support more maturing pups and yearlings, and thus increase their total reproductive output. In other words, its not that packs are large so that they can kill big prey, but rather big prey allows packs to get large. It reasonably follows that when food is scarce, pack size often decreases.

Finally, there may be some protective benefit to working together in a pack. Although there are occasional interactions with competing predator species (e.g., brown bears) that may require defense (see Chapter 9 – Other Species), most competition is among neighboring wolf packs. Group size is certainly one factor that tips the balance in any such interactions, though it seems unlikely that packs would remain large solely on the chance that they would win rare encounters with other packs or predators.

Not all packs are the same, however. They clearly vary in size among packs and over time, but they also vary in origin and composition, and many of the differences we see in wolf behavior are directly related to this variation. All packs are family groups of wolves. The so-called nuclear family consisting of parents and their offspring of one or more years (typical of a newly formed pack where unfamiliar breeders join and produce litters over several years) is the one most commonly assumed to be representative of wolves. However, the variations include an extended family (parents and one or more of their siblings, plus offspring), the disrupted family (one or both of the original parents missing), and the step-family (a disrupted family that has accepted an outside breeder). In all of these variations of the nuclear family the age and sex ratios of pack members, as well as their related, may vary substantially. For example, a relatively old pair of wolves (each 6-9 years old) may have had all of their offspring >2 years old disperse; when they have pups, there may only be one or two yearlings from the previous litter in the pack, and thus the age range is great. Conversely, a newly formed pair of dispersing yearlings may produce a litter of pups that are just two years younger than their parents. Similarly, the sex ratio may vary from an even split of half males and half females, to the case where one parent is the only member of their sex in the pack. Wolves other than breeders usually are related to one another as brothers and/or sisters, except in the cases where the pack has accepted an unrelated outside wolf as a breeder. In this case, subsequent pups would be half-brothers and half-sisters to previous pups. Breeders are rarely related to one another, and in fact are usually more closely related to members of neighboring packs (due to dispersal) than to their mates.

Pack sizes are usually reported as the maximum size of the family at a given time of the year. Over the course of the winter, when such counts are normally done, observers need to keep re-counting the pack because it is not uncommon for some pack members to be apart from the main part of their pack for hours or even days. Some members lag behind when traveling, others visit old kills, and some travel on their own, making exploratory excursions that often lead to dispersal. Packs also sometimes split for several days and hunt as separate units; this is particularly true for large packs (perhaps >12-15 wolves) and may occur on half of all hunts. In the summer wolf packs are even less cohesive because finding and catching prey is easier. Individual wolves often hunt on their own or with only one or two other pack mates. They regularly return to the den to bring back food to the nursing female and her growing pups, so contact with pack members if fairly frequent.

Another characteristic of packs is that their longevity is highly variable. In general, packs with a long lineage live in areas with a regularly available, predictable prey base, and where they experience relatively low mortality in any given year. Under these circumstances, pup production is steady, dispersal probably occurs routinely, clashes with adjacent packs are infrequent, and successful breeders live a long time (perhaps to age 10 or 11). The fewer disruptions there are to the pack's social structure, the longer it probably endures. Conversely, pack longevity is probably short where food sources are unpredictable or in short supply, thus causing adult wolves to die more frequently from inter-pack conflicts, more pups to die of starvation, and cause most young wolves to disperse as soon as they can.

Family Interactions

Growing Pups

Family members may prepare for pup care even before the pups are born. Some dens are dug in the fall, well before pups are to arrive, and whenever dens are dug, both adults and yearlings of both sexes may help with the digging and with providing food to the pregnant female. Though not all denning females do so, many have been observed to spend significant time in the den area for up to a month before giving birth, often accompanied by pack members.

Just before the time of parturition (birth), the pregnant female has usually ceased all efforts to forage for food and settles into the den. The actual birth of pups observed in captivity is much like that of domestic dogs. Once a pup is born, the female licks it and then nibbles at and consumes the membrane surrounding it. She noses the pup towards her belly and nipples; pups reflexively grab the nipple and suckle with an hour or two of birth. During the first week to 10 days, the tiny, close-eyed pups squirm and crawl on top of each other when they are not suckling, seeking the warmth of their mother, or sleeping. They clumsily roam the den chamber, bumping into the walls and each other before whimpering or crying out. The female often licks the pups' rear or

inguinal areas to get them to defecate and urinate; she consumes any milk feces produced until the pups are about 10-12 days of age, when they are large enough to see and walk to the den entrance and eliminate outside. At this age, they usually just scoot right back into the tunnel and den chamber and, as a result, no other adults have any real contact with the pups during these first few weeks, except for occasional visits by the father.

The pups continue to get more physically adept, and at about 3 weeks of age they really begin to experience the outside world by exploring, playing, and lying around in the open near the den entrance. Most importantly, they begin to interact with other pack members. They are still very attached to the actual den and spend significant time there, but they also are able to solicit play and care from older wolves. At this age, pups don't particularly care with whom they interact, as long as it's family. And at any sight of intruders, they dash back into the den for protection.

For family members other than the mother, their interactions with pups are key. During the summer when pups are growing and restricted to home sites, non-reproductive pack members care for pups by providing general defense from predators (e.g., vigilance, barking, and even attacking), and by bringing food back not only for the mother wolf, but for the pups, too. Pups are now able to ingest very small pieces of solid food, and a primary interaction of pups with other adults is soliciting food. The attendence of family members to pups needs may vary with sex, age, and social status, but any help they do give is likely to occur for several reasons. First, helping to assure the survival of closely related siblings may be the next best option for promoting their own genes (this is termed "kin selection"). They may also participate to enhance pack social bonds that are an important component of assuring their own survival. Finally, they may also participate in order to gain experience for when they become breeders.

At 3-4 weeks of age the pups are also large enough and able enough to suckle standing up. When hungry, usually about every 5

At 5 weeks of age, wolf pups are still small enough to be carried to new dens or home sites by their mothers, but large enough to move around on their own, as well. The pups' interactions with adults and other pups are essential in developing both motor and social skills.

hours, they make soft squeaks and approach their mother, then suckle for 3 minutes or so. After the age of 5 weeks, pups can move around on their own well enough, but they are still small enough for mothers to pick them up in their mouths to carry them. If a female changes dens or moves the pups to a rendezvous site during this time, she usually carries each pup to the new location. Non-nursing females, but not males, have been observed transporting pups this way, as well. When the mother of suckling pups interrupts nursing and trots away because of disturbance, the pups often follow at a short distance; this is likely a precursor to pups following older wolves leaving on a hunt.

During the next month or so, suckling bouts decrease in length and the interval between bouts increases until, at 10 weeks or so, wolf pups are fully weaned. During this time, solid food becomes a more and more important part of their diet. Their teeth are developing, as are their abilities to grab, tear, and chew meat. Growing pups may be able to forage for berries on their own at rendezvous sites, but because they cannot usually get meat on their own, they are dependent on family members to supply them. As a result, pups are extremely excited when an older wolf returns to the den from a hunt. The pups rush over and excitedly poke their muzzles around the adult's mouth. Assuming the wolf's stomach is full, this stimulus almost automatically results in the regurgitation of food; most regurgitations happen at the spot the pups first meet the returning provider. Pups grab whatever they can as fast as they can, then often scamper off to consume their prize. A large piece of food may end up in a tug-of-war between pups, and excess food is subsequently gathered and stored by the pups in caches around the den site. Some of the regurgitated food certainly makes its way to a mother wolf tending her pups, and much of the cached food is probably eaten by whichever hungry pack members subsequently find it.

Play is an important component of pup life. When not sleeping or eating, the pups' main interactions with other pups and with older wolves are through play. Most play does not result in the kind of dominance behaviour that are seen when pups are contesting for food; rather, play seems to be a cohesive social force. Play in wolf pups is much of what we see in dogs. There are clearly behaviors such as stalking, pouncing, and chasing that will be used in other contexts in the future. We recognize bowing, tail-wagging, grinning, and head-tossing as communication signals. Play such as leaps and bouncy galloping seems exaggerated and pleasurable, and play reversals (e.g., chaser to chased) would seem to encourage more intensive socialization. Pups may play tag or keep-away, or may wrestle tumble for hours on end. All of this play helps to strengthen the social bondings of the pack mates.

Hunting clearly is an important survival skill for growing pups to learn. This includes finding prey and knowing how to kill it safely. To start of with, wolf pups are born with the propensity to chase and capture small moving animals, like mice, and young pups have been observed to "mouse-pounce". At the age of 3 months, pups may move up to 500 m (0.3 mi) away from a home site on their own, even to another nearby den or rendezvous site. They also may follow older wolves for a short distance, and if by chance some prey animal is roused, they will chase it. By the age of 4 months, however, pups are capable of traveling for even longer distances and they actually begin to accompany older wolves on hunts. They are clearly not done growing (see Chapter 2 – Morphology), but they are ready to learn the finer points of making a living as a wolf. Because wolves travel so much on such hunts, we can mostly only speculate about the ways in which pups actually learn to hunt successfully. They certainly must follow older wolves closely, recognize when prey is scented, and join in on chases. Though they undoubtedly watch prey being caught by others, some must just pounce and try to grab on. In the course of these attacks, I suspect young wolves learn via the "school of hard knocks" how dangerous prey can be, and with each attempt become more savvy about the timing and cooperation needed to kill something as large as a deer or elk. Success certainly reinforces specific behaviors, maybe even innovative ones. But once wolves find out what works, it is likely that they stick with tried and true techniques throughout their lives.

By the time wolf pups are 8 months old, they are nearly the size of adults, and at age 10 months may be physiologically able to breed (though they rarely or ever do so in the wild — see Chapter 7 — Populations). Full-grown pups in a pack of wolves seen traveling together in the winter can sometimes only be identified by their playful behavior (in contrast to the purposeful pace of older wolves). For the most part, however, these young wolves have entered into the world of adulthood. Though at times the family may treat them with some forgiveness, most of the time they are required to act their size, if not their age.

Among Adults

The social relationship among "adult" wolves is a mix of behaviors reflecting both conflict and cohesion. Given that individuals must first ensure their own survival, conflicts within a pack are inevitable. To be an evolutionary success, a wolf must secure food resources in the short term and mating opportunities in the long term. When such valuable but often limited resources are up for grabs, physical or emotional battles are sure to arise. At the same time, most wolves are members of a social group that often seems to operate at an optimal level when the ability and opportunity to cooperate, or at least get along well, is high. This group cohesiveness is a hallmark of the species, and it certainly coexists with, and necessarily complements, conflict.

Traditionally, the social organization of wolves has been depicted as a pair of linear dominance hierarchies, or pecking orders within each sex. In this traditional view of social order, the most dominant male wolf is called the "alpha" male, the second most dominant the "beta", and the one that is least likely to win any confrontation, the "omega". The female hierarchy mirrors this ranking. We thought that the alpha wolves were the biggest, strongest, breeding wolves

that lead the pack and assured its survival, and that constant testing and even small battles determined this order. Also, it was most often presumed that this dominance was determined prior to birth (i.e., is genetic) and revealed itself fully in the course of the interactions among pups, and then within the entire pack.

It turns out, however, that this is a simplified version of what really goes on in a pack. First of all, there is no good evidence that leaders of wolf packs are destined from birth to do so. There may be nutritional conditions that help a certain pup grow bigger faster, and this in turn may help secure a dominant role among siblings. Perhaps other, more dominant wolves leave the pack or even get killed, thus opening up an opportunity for another wolf to assume a dominant position. Or it may turn out that a wolf with the social skills to best maintain pack cohesion turns out to be a pack leader. The point is that relative dominance of wolves certainly can change with circumstance over time, and is not predestined.

Second, dominance hierarchies do exist in packs, but they are mostly the result of natural family relationships. In packs composed of both parents and successive offspring, the parents are biggest for a long while, and intimidating relationships between them are a necessity that is established from birth. Older brothers and sisters also have more experience than younger ones (but not as much as their parents) and it is natural that, up to a point, these older and bigger siblings generally win out in social conflicts over younger ones. Thus the hierarchy is really a result mostly of age; it hasn't been determined solely through innumerable tests of will and strength.

There are of course packs that have not resulted from successive production of litters of a pair of wolves. These step-families includes in immigrant breeder that must establish a social position without the benefit of a long-term relationship with pack members. In these circumstances, it might take more obvious and more numerous aggressive interactions to maintain breeding status. It has been captive packs formed under these, or even more complicated, circumstances that, in the past, lead scientists to emphasize dominance hierarchies as an important and constant social condition of packs.

Watching pack member's social behaviour in the wild, however, paints a different picture. Conflicts occur very rarely compared to the normal "cohesive" behaviors of the pack. Wild wolves are amazingly non-aggressive in their interactions, and even though there might be wolves that are obviously followed on hunts, those that are first to bite into prey, and those that do all of the breeding, social life in a wild wolf pack seems relatively benign. Subtle signs are exchanged vocally or olfactorily, body posture and position indicate the degree to which interactions are to be initiated or avoided, and tolerance of the young seems high. This high amount of cooperative behavior makes sense; it is energetically inefficient to spend time on unnecessary conflict, and sometimes even dangerous. The only times it does make sense is, as noted above, when food resources or mating opportunities are in relatively short supply. This is when dominance is an important survival attribute, not only among pack members, but among non-pack members, as well.

Non-family Interactions

As noted in Chapter 5 – Land Use, wolves dependent on non-migratory prey are almost always territorial. Packs defend their home range through a variety of visual, olfactory, and vocal signs, and (rarely) through direct physical conflict, as well. In general, wolves don't tolerate wolves if they are not members of their pack. They have their own resources that they depend on, and they don't want other wolves to have access to them. Wolves normally respect each other's boundaries, and a long-running truce of sorts typifies the wolf community. A result of this type of sociality is that the boundaries of wolf territories don't often have much wolf activity in them. Other than marking them on a fairly regular basis (see Chapter 4 – Communication), these territory edges are not places where packs seem to spend much time. This

is because if they did they would increase the chances of physical contact with a neighboring pack; wolves generally avoid such direct contact because the consequences can be so severe. As a result, the edges of wolf territories serve as buffer zones between packs. They are the "cushion" that allows packs to live next door to one another without constant battling. A further consequence of this behavior is that prey species and other carnivores find these boundary areas a better place to live, because wolves spend less time there than they do in the middle of their territories.

This territorial coexistence breaks down, however, when food resources are diminished. Wolves need to eat to survive, and in the event that prey is so scarce that hunting becomes less and less successful, wolves will "trespass" into a neighboring pack's territory. Sometimes they seem to know that their neighbors are on the far side of the territory, and that it may be easy to sneak in and "raid the larder". Perhaps they can detect very fresh scent marks and know from experience that it will be awhile before the marks are freshened. Other times, though, packs that trespass get caught, and then mortal battles take place. Wolves are sometimes chased, grabbed, and killed in the most aggressive kind of dominance displays. They are rarely actually eaten by other wolves, but this is territorial defense at its most severe.

Because not all wolves are territorial year-round, some interactions between packs are less aggressive. Wolf packs that follow migratory prey often find themselves in areas where just the previous day another pack may have been. When prey animals become concentrated in winter, several packs may even live in a relatively small area simultaneously. Under these circumstances, packs appear to be more tolerant of one another. They keep their distance from other packs and seemingly respect the sanctity of kill sites. Despite the proximity between packs that would trigger major fights in territorial circumstances, in these places, the packs adjust their behavior to assure survival.

Dispersal

Most wolves disperse from their natal pack when they become physiologically mature under conditions where no breeding opportunities are present. They set out either to find a mate in the same circumstances, or to find a pack in need of a breeder. Sometimes they leave the pack temporarily and then return, only to leave again (up to a total of 6 times before making a final break); other times the first excursion out of the territory is their last.

To understand the social context in which wolves disperse, a review of the specifics of dispersers can be helpful. First of all, dispersal is not sex-biased; that is, wolves of either sex have an equal propensity to leave their pack. Second, wolves as young as 5 months of age and as old as 5 years of age have dispersed from natal packs, though the most common age class of dispersers is yearlings (12-24 months old). Wolves most commonly disperse by themselves, though they have been known to leave with one and even two same-aged siblings. Dispersers of any age generally do so either during the late winter and early spring, in the months just preceding the denning season, or during the late fall and early winter, prior to the breeding season.

These peaks suggest that a major trigger to dispersal is social competition. In anticipation of new pups, recently bred wolves may be more aggressive in their defense of each other and of their food resources. Females need to increase their body fat for lactation, and males need to safeguard their reproductive investment. For wolves that are newly capable of breeding, social interactions with such wolves may elevate to the point where coexistence is difficult, thus leading to a choice of dispersing alone. For reproductively capable wolves that choose to stay with the pack, it may turn out that by the next fall, increasing hormone levels are such that the reproductive urge is even stronger, and the need to find a mate under circumstances outside the natal pack are intense; thus, there is a seasonal increase in dispersal prior to the breeding season, as well.

Another major factor contributing to increased dispersal rates is food. When food supplies are relatively high, dispersal rates seem lower than when they are scarce. Food competition seems to enhance the urge to disperse, with food-stressed animals more willing to take the chance of leaving, finding a mate, and locating alternative food resources in what is likely unknown territory. This idea that the relative amount of food availability is important to wolf dispersal is supported by the observation that wolf dispersal rates are higher when there is an opportunity to recolonize an area. Prey densities may actually be higher in a natal territory than in an unoccupied territory elsewhere, but they would have to be shared with pack mates at home. In a new location, prey only need be shared with a new mate, and thus relatively speaking food is no less abundant. This, combined with the opportunity to breed, is what encourages dispersal.

Finally, it may be that detection of a potential mate at the edge of one's territory is a big incentive to disperse. Some monitored wolves that dispersed from their natal range found mates quickly; others that may have dispersed for different reasons and did not immediately find a mate at a territory edge, often travelled alone for much longer.

Of course, in addition to finding another wandering disperser of the opposite sex and settling down somewhere, dispersing wolves can obtain mates in other ways. Presumably, they could find a pack and drive out or kill an already established breeder, but this seems very risky. It could probably also join a pack, find a mate, and then disperse again with that mate, but again it seems unlikely that a wolf would happen to find an extra, capable, but non-breeding mate on any regular basis without encountering a strong anti-intruder reaction from a pack. More likely, a disperser might be able to locate a breeder in need of a mate through olfactory or even vocal means, and with careful interactions with the pack, be able to join it and take over the role of step-parent and breeder. In any case, various kinds and intensities of social interactions among wolves are clearly essential elements of successful dispersal.

Populations:
What is a Wolf Population and How Does it Change?

Imagine that you are flying in a small plane over the Bialowieza Forest in eastern Poland in late May. The Forest, which extends into Belarus, is a large, mostly protected natural area that has a full European complement of predators and their prey. You look down into in a small clearing and see three wolves curled up, seeming to enjoy a warm, sunny afternoon. The plane banks to fly over the clearing again and at the edge, under a pine tree, you spot the den. It's a large hole in the ground that was freshly dug this spring, with trampled dirt spreading out in a fan towards the middle of the clearing. As you come around to get a better look, you see four, no five, no six small pups tumble out of the hole into the sunshine. One of the adults gets up, stretches, and slowly walks over the pups to nuzzle them. This pack of three has just grown to nine, and the Forest continues its legacy of providing good wolf habitat.

Every spring when pups are born, wolf packs have the potential to nearly double in size. Usually they don't, and by the next spring the population may not even be as big as it was the year before. The study of such changes in animal numbers is referred to as the field of population dynamics, and it encompasses both a description of population change and the analysis of the underlying reasons for change. In the case of wolves, this process usually means repeatedly counting them, following the fates of individuals, and monitoring their environment, especially their prey, for years on end.

Wolves do not occur everywhere within their range. A first step in understanding wolf population dynamics is to identify the places where they do occur and compare them with places where they do not. Trying to document their presence in any one particular spot, however, is difficult because wolves are so elusive and wide-ranging. More difficult still is documenting that a "population" of wolves exists. Identifying a population is hard, in part, because the tracks or sightings one collects may be of one errant wolf that has roamed hundreds of kilometers from the next nearest pack, and not evidence of a pack. Even a pack of wolves does not necessarily make a population. At a minimum, several packs usually need to be in contact with one another to be called a population, which entails being able to sustain itself. Since in many places within wolf range such a minimum number of packs does not occur, one must eventually wonder what it is about a place that allows a wolf population to exist.

As it turns out, the abundance and availability of food (for wolves this means hoofed prey such as red deer or moose) dictate the potential for wolves to inhabit an area. Given relatively higher ungulate populations, wolves have more opportunities to catch prey, and as we will see, the availability of food ultimately affects nutritional levels and thus wolf reproduction, survival, and behavior. Prey availability is related not only to abundance, but also to the vulnerability of prey. Deep snow or disease may make some prey more vulnerable, and thus more "available", than others (see Chapter 8 – Food). If enough prey is available to wolves, and the area is big enough to support several packs, then a population may be present.

In addition to prey, however, human behaviors that result in excessive direct or indirect killing of wolves may influence where and in what numbers wolves occur. Human attitudes and traditions have played a major role determining the locations of wolf populations, because in the past, unrelenting persecution of wolves by humans has resulted in their complete elimination from some areas. Today, wolves thrive in remote areas where human

Wolf numbers sometimes change dramatically from year to year, depending on food sources, weather, and various causes of death.

density is low, or in designated wilderness areas, national parks, and wildlife refuges where wolves are protected. Even where humans are more common, wolf populations can exist if purposeful killing by hunting or trapping is regulated, and where illegal or accidental killing of wolves by humans is low.

Finally, wolf populations may persist in marginal habitats (i.e., where food resources are poor, perhaps because of competition with humans, and/or where there is high human-caused mortality) because dispersing wolves from adjacent "source" populations can supplement some losses. Wolves disperse readily and can move to new areas fairly easily (see Chapter 5 – Land Use). Thus, the distance one wolf population is located relative to the next nearest one plays an important role in wolf population distribution.

Abundance

Estimating Numbers

Even if we know a wolf population probably occurs in an area, how do we know how many wolves live there? Hunters, trappers, and more recently, biologists, have been trying to figure their abundance for a long time. From repeated observations throughout the year over very large areas, they know that populations are comprised of many packs, or families, of wolves, as well as a good number of "floaters", or lone wolves. They have counted adults and pups, inventoried changes in pack size and composition, and found innumerable carcasses. More recently (in the past 35 years), biologists have attached collars with small radio-transmitters to and then intensively monitored literally thousands of wild wolves in many different circumstances around the world. This technique gives many details on their movements, reproduction, and survival. The sum of this traditional and scientific ecological knowledge has resulted in a fairly clear understanding of what a wolf population is and how it changes.

First of all, the packs that make up a wolf population vary in size from just 2 wolves up to 25 or more. However, the average pack size is usually 3 to 8, and does not differ significantly among wolf populations, even when their major prey is different (i.e., packs feeding mainly on elk are not larger than those feeding on wild boar). Overall, pack size also does not vary with prey density; packs, on average, are just as large in areas where many prey as where there are fewer.

Packs are obviously largest just after pups are born; this is the major annual increment to wolf populations. As the summer progresses, some pups and adults die, reducing overall pack size, and mortality of adults typically increases during the fall and winter (see below). Fall and winter are also the major times of wolf dispersal, and thus packs may become smaller as individual pack members leave. During this period, some wolves may also join packs, and single wolves pair with other wolves, especially just before and during the breeding season in February, so pack sizes in winter can fluctuate somewhat.

Of course, not all wolves live in packs. At any one time, some wolves that have dispersed from packs are traveling alone, or if with another wolf, may not have settled in a territory. One lone female wolf in north-central Minnesota seemed to defend a territory by herself for most of the winter before she finally paired up with a mate. The proportion of these wolves in a population varies seasonally, as do dispersal rates and the rates at which individuals settle into territories, but on average these wolves comprise about 10-15% of a wolf population.

To census a wolf population, one has to make an assumption that the packs are territorial, and that these territories form a sort of mosaic on the landscape. Through repeated observation of packs, and identification of individual packs by their location and composition (e.g., a maximum of 6 black and 2 gray wolves always south of the river vs. 2 black and 7 gray wolves north of the river), a map of packs can be drawn, and the entire area in which they occur can be identified. A total count of pack wolves can be made, and to that an estimated number of lone wolves can be

Just as the size of wolf packs varies, so does the density of wolves. Much of wolf density is influenced simply by the variation in food availability, which across wolves' wide geographic range can vary more than 10-fold. Increased mortality can drive wolf numbers lower, but relatively abundant food increases pup production and survival.

added. As an example, in an area of 3,300 km² (1,980 mi²), 12 packs of wolves ranging in size from 4-9 might total 77 individuals. If lone wolves made up about 13% of the population, then the population would number 77 + 6 = 83, and the wolf density in the area would be 26/1,000 km² (67/1,000 mi²).

Variation in Density

Wolf densities naturally vary tremendously, however. It is not uncommon for studies in the far north of Canada and Russia to record densities of healthy wolf populations of <5/1,000 km² (<13/1,000 mi²). In contrast, maximum wolf densities are over an order of magnitude higher. In my study in north-central Minnesota during the 1980s, I recorded densities of 69 wolves/1,000 km² (179/1,000 mi²) in early winter, and 50/1,000 km² (129/1,000 mi²) in late winter. On Isle Royale in Lake Superior (Canada-U.S. border) wolf density exceeded 80/1,000 km² (207/1,000 mi²) during the 1970's and reached 92/1,000 km² (238/1,000 mi²) in 1980. In general, however, maximum mid-winter wolf densities measured for mainland population over a number of years have rarely measured more than 40/1,000 km² (100/1,000 mi²).

It turns out that at least 60-70% of the variation in wolf density in all of North America, and probably the world, is directly accounted for simply by the variation in food availability. This relationship is derived from more than 30 intensive studies which identified the total average ungulate biomass (often >1 ungulate species) present and the average wolf densities for periods of several consecutive years. The relationship between prey abundance and wolf numbers may vary for areas with migratory versus non-migratory prey, or where prey concentrate seasonally, but nevertheless, there are no indications that, over time, wolf numbers are mostly limited by anything other than ungulate numbers and availability.

The rest of the variation in wolf density is mostly related to their survival and mortality rates, but it is definitely influenced by prey availability. Ungulate biomass might be relatively high compared to wolf density (lots of food per wolf) either where wolves are heavily exploited (low wolf survival and thus relatively low density) or where newly protected wolf populations are recolonizing former range (low wolf density due to previous over exploitation). This is so because such wolf populations have not had the chance to grow to their "maximum" size or number relative to food availability. Conversely, food abundance may seem relatively low for unexploited wolf populations (were individual wolf survival is high) or those where ungulates are heavily harvested (low survival, and thus low numbers, of ungulates). These wolf populations have reached or surpassed their maximum size, and prey is relatively scarce (food per wolf is low).

Changes in wolf density within a single study area also have been attributed to changing densities of prey or changing survival rates. In long-term studies in northeast Minnesota, Isle Royale, and southwest Quebec, wolf numbers changed as a direct result of changes in deer or moose numbers. The response of individual wolf populations to this change, however, seems to be like that for other cyclic mammals; when ungulate numbers change, a change in wolf density seems to lag a few years. For example, when moose densities on Isle Royale increased due to mild winters and lots of available food, it took several years for the wolf population to increase at the same rate. When the moose population crashed after a very severe winter, the wolves hung on for a year or two, but then plunged, as well. Wolf densities in an area have also varied when they were heavily harvested and then were allowed to recover. In Yukon, Canada and in Alaska, wolves were intentionally reduced to low numbers for up to six years in a row to allow their prey populations to increase. Subsequently, these low wolf populations were allowed to recover, and their numbers have increased rapidly because the relative numbers of prey, which in the meantime had increased substantially, was very high.

Population Demography

In order to understand the way in which food or mortality cause changes in wolf numbers, a detailed assessment of wolf population demography is needed. Demography is the description of the factors that are key to populations and include reproduction, survival, and dispersal.

Reproduction

There are recorded instances of wolves in captivity being capable of breeding at 9-10 months of age, and several 2-year-old captive wolves have produced pups. Prior to the mid-1980s, however, the youngest wild female wolf known to have produced pups was 3 years old. Since then, at least two known 2-year-old wolves in north-central Minnesota produced pups, as did one in Alaska. In the wild then, mating probably first occurs no earlier than age 22 months, reproduction no earlier than age 2. Few wolves live longer than four or five years, but a female wolf 11 years old has been known to produce pups. There is no evidence that females reach reproductive senescence before they die, but at least one female wolf in the Arctic stopped breeding when her daughter took over that role in the pack.

Even though most adult female wolves are capable of producing pups every year, not all do so. Most wolf packs produce only one litter of pups per year, though two litters per pack have been reported. Consequently, if there are more than 2 wolves >2 years old per pack, some do not breed, and populations with larger packs have a lower proportion of breeders. On the Kenai Peninsula in Alaska, increased harvest resulted in smaller packs and territories, and establishment of new packs in vacated areas. As a result, breeders comprised a higher proportion of the population and the rate of pup production increased. There are no really good explanations as to why packs in some areas, e.g., Denali Park, Alaska, more frequently have 2 females in the pack that produce pups. Pack sizes are not necessarily greater in these areas compared with other similar areas with similar prey bases. It does seem that the percent of wolves in a population that reproduce is a function of pack age structure, size, and number of packs vs. lone wolves in the population and, as noted earlier (see Chapter 6 – Social Behavior) pack composition, but not all of these factors have been confirmed as being contributory.

Although the sex ratio of any one litter of wolf pups may vary from all males to all females, the ratio for an entire population always seems to come out at about 50:50. Litter size usually averages 4-6 pups, regardless of the age of the mother. However, litters were small for an unexploited population in Ontario (average = 4.9) but large for exploited populations in Alaska (6.5) and northeastern Minnesota (6.4). This suggests that litter size may increase with greater ungulate biomass per wolf. More recent data strongly confirm this assertion, with litter sizes increasing 50% with a 6-fold increase in ungulate biomass available per wolf. It seems logical that mothers that are very well fed may actually ovulate more eggs, may be able to provide more resources per fetus, and thus give birth to more pups. Again, food resources seem a most important factor in wolf demography.

A consequence of newborn pups being added to the population each spring is that adults and yearlings usually comprise 55-75% of all pack members. Limited data indicates that of the adults and yearlings, there is either an equal sex ratio, or one with slightly more females. Populations with the highest proportion of pups in packs are usually those whose numbers have been reduced substantially, possibly through some disease outbreak or more commonly via control efforts by humans, thus leaving only small packs or pairs. When these groups produce an average litter of pups, surviving pups can clearly make up a high proportion of the pack. Similarly, a population of wolves recolonizing an area has ample opportunity to form new packs comprised only of pairs of wolves, and newborn pups may be relatively abundant in this circumstance, too.

Survival and Mortality

Survival of pups in summer is difficult to measure, but data strongly suggest that survival is directly related to food abundance. Summer pup survival was almost double in one area where the amount of prey available to adults was four times greater (89% in Alaska vs. 48% in Minnesota). In a long-term study in northeastern Minnesota, pup survival decreased over time, likely in response to a declining numbers of deer. Also, the percent of pups in fall or winter populations correlates to food abundance, and the percent of pups in the population or in packs is highest in newly-protected and heavily-exploited populations. These situations likely reflect both large litters and higher pup survival where food abundance is high.

In comparison with yearlings and adults, pup survival rates are low in summer. Few wolves in these older age classes die then, and their summer survival rates are almost always greater than 90%. During winter, however, the survival rate of pups is equal to or only slightly lower than that of yearlings and adults. There is no evidence that female wolf survival differs from that of males. Overall, documented yearling and adult wolf annual survival rates in remote wilderness or in protected areas vary from about 55 to 85%. On average, in a population that does not change in overall numbers from year to year, annual survival of adult-size wolves is about 65%. This means that each year 35% of adult wolves die, and yet the population remains the same because the production of pups makes up for this loss.

In the few studies where it has been documented, dispersing wolves seem to have lower survival than do wolves of the same age that remain in packs. Dispersing wolves travel through new areas, are not familiar with the distribution of prey, and must work harder to maintain their condition. They also are less familiar with the distribution of other wolves that may kill them, or may be more likely to get hit by a vehicle or to meet humans that may kill them.

Wolves die from a variety of natural factors. The role of diseases such as rabies, canine distemper, and parvovirus, and parasites such as heartworm and sarcoptic mange might be important causes of death, but documentation is somewhat lacking. As far as accidents go, adult wolves have died from kicks in the head or body by deer, moose, and musk ox, and they have even been trampled by large prey. Wolves have been known to fall over cliffs while chasing sheep and to die in avalanches in the high mountains. Adult wolves have few natural predators (perhaps tigers in the Russian Far East), though brown bears and even black bears probably kill some pups. Starvation mainly affects pups, especially when prey is relatively scarce. Adults wolves also may starve to death, though this is more likely for injured wolves that are on their own without pack mates to help them with hunting.

Wolves killing wolves is the most important mortality factor for wolf populations that are not affected by humans. Such deaths occur in remote or protected areas because these populations are often as dense as food supplies allow. Consequently, any decrease in prey availability (i.e., lower prey numbers or an increase in conditions where prey is hard to catch; see Chapter 8 – Food) causes wolves to search outside their territory more often and trespass into other territories. As trespassing increases, so does the chance of fatal encounters with other wolves.

Humans have killed wolves for a long time. Historically, wolves were shot and trapped for utilitarian purposes, and poisoned when total elimination was intended (see Chapter 10 – Humans). Over 100 years ago, the U.S. government authorized the elimination of wolves in Yellowstone National Park in order to protect big game species, and by the 1920s the government trappers had finished their job. In recent decades, legal and illegal shooting and trapping, incidental trapping, depredation control, and vehicle accidents have been responsible for most human-caused deaths of wolves. Focused programs to kill wolves to increase prey numbers have reduced wolf populations in Alaska by over 60% in some years, and in a few site-specific control areas even eliminated entire packs. Even in legally protected populations in the north-central part of the U.S., human-caused wolf deaths reached 20-30% annually just 10 year ago.

Many of the human-caused deaths in protected populations occur because wolves kill domestic livestock. The government control program in Minnesota, for example, accounted for the deaths of more than 161 wolves there in 1998. Even though this control was targeted only at farms where depredation had occurred, it amounted to about 7% of the entire wolf population in the state. Private citizens also kill wolves illegally to protect livestock, pets, and even deer, or even just for the thrill of it. Wolves also are killed accidentally by vehicles or are captured in traps or snares set for other species. Some are mistakenly shot as coyotes, but historically these sources of death have been lower than intentional killing.

In examining the more recent demise of wolves in the U.S, a study in Wisconsin revealed that wolves had not survived in areas with high road densities. Subsequent field studies elsewhere supported that conclusion in general, though some established wolf populations do live where road and human population densities are somewhat higher than where wolves were eliminated historically. Road density, however, remains the best indicator of potential wolf habitat in many places, and most wolves there seem to settle where road densities are relatively low. Roads are important because they might change wolf behavior, because some additional traffic might mean increased collisions between vehicles and wolves, and most importantly because roads allow human access and that could facilitate intentional killings. Roads and human population density are only indices to the amount of human activity in an area and do not reflect the changes over time in human attitudes or in law enforcement activities. Because the actual pressure on wolves

from being killed by humans is likely decreasing as attitudes become more favorable towards wolves, it is not surprising that wolves are expanding their range in many areas. They are successfully occupying areas where road and human densities once were thought to have been too high.

Dispersal and Immigration

Dispersal rates of wolves vary by age. In general, about 16% of pups alive in the fall will disperse before their first birthday. Of the remaining pups that become yearlings, another 52% disperse some time before they turn 2 years old. Finally, about 10% of the remaining adults will eventually disperse, often sooner than later. This behavior adds up to a high proportion of wolves leaving packs, and thus a high "turnover" rate in the population. It seems there are always wolves leaving packs, exploring near and far, and sometimes finding a place to settle down or to join another pack. Undoubtedly, a few wolves that avoid dying too soon end up roaming for months or even years before finding a mate or a pack.

Because dispersal is the means by which wolves become reproductively active in new areas, this behavior is important to wolf population dynamics. Dispersing wolves serve as the excess individuals from "source" populations that sustain "sink" populations. In the case of wolf populations that have been intentionally reduced, much of the subsequent increase in wolf numbers has been through immigration. This is especially true where entire packs have been eliminated, and thus immigrant pairs of wolves find ideal circumstances under which to start up their own pack. Because dispersing wolves establish territories or join packs anywhere from immediately adjacent to their natal pack to perhaps 50-100 km and farther away (see Chapter 5 – Land Use), "connectivity" of source and sink populations can be relatively high, even over large geographic scales.

Also, dispersing wolves serve to expand their species' geographic range. In the last 20 years, wolves have naturally expanded their

*Most wolves disperse from their natal packs, sometime before their first birthday and
usually by age 2, resulting in a relatively high turnover in packs. When they leave, they walk, trot, run,
and swim to find a new area, and a mate, in which to settle and raise a new generation of wolves.*

range in countries such as Italy, Poland and the U.S., and have even recolonized countries such as Germany and France. More pointedly, reintroduction of wolves in several parts of the U.S. has lead to quickly expanding populations in the mountainous West. In all of these circumstances, relatively abundant prey, low human-caused mortality rates, and adjacent source populations have allowed new packs to become established and to thrive.

Rates of Change

The maximum reported rate of annual wolf population increase over a period of several years is about 50% (e.g., from 20 to 30, 30 to 45, and 45 to 66 over a 3-year interval). This rate of change has occurred both where wolves are naturally recolonizing areas and where they are repopulating areas where humans systematically removed them. Given this high rate of increase, and assuming that food would not limit population growth for a number of years, the wolf population in such areas grows rapidly. The main component of dramatic increases in wolf numbers is usually reproduction. Packs of 2-4 wolves successfully raising 2-4 pups can theoretically double or triple their numbers in a single year. However, depending on the reproductive status of wolf populations in surrounding areas, immigration also may provide a major role in population increases.

For any wolf population the observed annual rate of change (given an adequate food base) is most directly related to overall mortality. Although natural causes of mortality may have significant effects on wolf numbers, it is primarily human-caused mortality that makes populations change the most. Human exploitation of wolf populations affects rates of increase by changing densities and thus per-capita food resources. Potential rates of increase should be higher after exploitation because increased per capita food availability will result in increased pup production and survival; however, exploitation rates may be too high to be fully compensated by reproduction (i.e., a "sink"), and

thus these populations are only sustained through immigration. The maximum sustainable rate of exploitation is probably not much more than 30% of the early winter population. This proportion comes from a number of studies, both in natural populations and those where human-caused mortality was high, by comparing mortality rates and subsequent population changes over time.

Population Persistence

Wolf persistence on a small scale is limited primarily by the amount of available land that contains enough prey to support at least one pack. More importantly, a single, isolated pack may have a lower chance of surviving than a group of several adjacent packs. Theoretically, the chances of an isolated pack avoiding some demographic catastrophe (e.g., a very skewed sex ratio) or difficulties from inbreeding vary directly with its distance or degree of isolation (e.g., access to natural travel corridor) from the next nearest pack or packs.

However, with abundant and available food resources and no human-caused deaths, a small population on Isle Royale resulting from a single pack has survived for 50 years, even at the expense of an estimated 50% loss of genetic variability. Also, parvovirus was unintentionally introduced to the island and did contribute to a population crash and total lack of successful reproduction for a number of years. Still, the population persists.

The smallest demographically viable population might include two to three adjacent packs of perhaps four wolves each. The packs could persist anywhere ungulate prey occurred at the specified biomass density, and where mortality was less than net reproduction. One might also hope that these packs were not too closely related, a result of being not too far from other wolves (40-60 km2) and thus able to "exchange" breeders every so often. In time, these isolated packs would be the source for dispersers that end up expanding, and not just maintaining, the population.

Food:
What do Wolves Eat?

Although wolves are big carnivores that can chase down the swiftest of prey, they also are canids, the group of carnivores that seems best adapted (via teeth, digestive system, and physical capabilities) to take advantage of the widest variety of food types. This flexibility, combined with the extremely wide geographic distribution of wolves, suggests that their diet probably is neither simple nor very predictable. Not surprisingly, wolves everywhere eat myriad animals and a fair amount of plant material, limited in variety only by what is present at a given time or place. As has been noted before, the most accurate statement that can be made about the diet of wolves is that it is usually hard-won and highly variable.

Food Habits

Identification

Humans have known something about what wolves eat ever since they made contact. Early on, humans possibly found and then scavenged the remains of prey killed by wolves. Since these carcasses were probably those of large mammals, they certainly did not represent the whole of wolf diet; in hindsight, however, they likely indicated the most important kinds prey for wolves.

Subsequently, humans and wolves have had direct contact in a variety of more intense and often conflicting ways (see Chapter 10 – Humans). More specifically, for thousands of years human hunters have competed directly with wolves for food. Because of their extraordinary observational skills, hunters probably long ago obtained traditional knowledge about what wolves eat. Biologists have simply adapted the skills used in gathering such knowledge into a more scientific framework to be able to describe the diet of wolves in more detail.

Whether in summer or winter, carcasses of wolf-killed prey may be most easily found by watching for ravens and other scavenging birds which are obvious when they congregate at kills. Some ravens even follow hunting wolves in anticipation of a meal (see Chapter 9 – Species Interactions). Carcasses can also be found by following tracks of wolves, which is easy on fresh snow. Since most of the geographic range of wolves lies in areas that receive snow in winter, this is a commonly used technique nearly everywhere. When wolf tracks are intercepted, they are followed forward and/or backwards until a kill site is found. Given the long distances that wolves often travel between successful kills, following tracks on the ground, can be exhausting. In some places, either fixed-wing aircraft or helicopters are used to speed up the tracking and the finding of kills by identifying blood in the snow. However, this can be difficult or even impossible in heavily forested areas and detailed information on unsuccessful hunting attempts cannot be readily gathered. Also, the opportunity to track is only present until the next snowfall.

For wolves preying on large ungulates, such as moose, it also may be possible to gather a complete record of wolf kills not by continuously following tracks, but more simply by locating a pack (containing one or more radio-marked individuals) once or twice a day for a period of time. In fact, I did this for two consecutive winters in northern Alberta, Canada. Every morning during February and March, I flew with a skilled pilot to find a pack of 9-13 wolves that lived near the Athabasca River. If they weren't at a carcass, and they hadn't been at a carcass the day before, I flew again in the afternoon to find them. By this method, I believe I located every moose that the wolves killed during those months. On several mornings the weather was bad and I could not fly until the afternoon, and I missed one or two days completely during each 2-month interval. Once I only just found the remains of a 200-kg (440-lb) calf moose because one radio-collared member of the pack stayed an extra 15 minutes at the carcass after the others had left. Overall, however, my record was likely complete, or nearly so, and the data I obtained were unique at the time.

Tracking works well in the winter, particularly when snowfalls are regular, but what about in the summer? Sometimes in the summer individual wolves are frequently located at carcasses, but because the pack often is not traveling as a group, it is difficult to know what the others are doing. Also, one study found that by checking each summer kill on the ground, many were in fact carcasses from the previous winter to which wolves had returned. Also, the diet of wolves is much more varied in summer than in winter, and thus identifying foods by following wolves in summer is often a fruitless exercise.

Another means of identifying wolf foods in both winter and summer is by examining stomach contents. This was popular when many wolves were hunted or trapped, and carcasses were usually available. It also worked best in winter, when frozen carcasses/stomachs could keep for a long while. In contrast, it is easy to understand that any samples collected in summer would be few; wolves are more rarely killed in summer because they are too hard to find and their pelts are worthless. Samples would be more difficult to deal with in warm weather because they would deteriorate so quickly. Stomach contents are still examined in some studies, particularly when specific food items such as livestock remains indicate if a wolf killed for livestock depredations was indeed eating domestic animals.

The most ubiquitous and relatively unbiased means of describing the diet of wolves is to carefully examine the contents of wolf feces, more commonly referred to as "scats". Most scats are relatively dry when excreted (see Chapter 2 – Morphology) and are comprised of indigestible remains of prey such as bone and hair. As such, they are useful study items for three reasons. Scats hold together fairly well for many days or weeks, and even for months in the winter. Thus, they are a record of consumed food that doesn't disappear as quickly as tracks or other signs, and

a good sample of them collected even at infrequent intervals can be illustrative. Also, it turns out that the contents of scats are fairly easily identified. Though bones are often crunched beyond recognition, the hairs of mammalian prey all have species-specific scale patterns on their surface that can be identified microscopically. Many hairs can be identified by eye once a reference collection or key is used and an identifier gets some practice. Similarly, bird feathers, insect remains, seeds, and some vegetation are fairly easy to identify with practice. And sometimes, little practice is needed to identify the contents of the cobalt-blue, semi-liquid scats that one wolf pup we caught at a blueberry patch was producing. Finally, substantial samples of scats may be gathered fairly easily. Because of the concentration of wolf activity near dens and rendezvous sites, it is not uncommon to be able to collect hundreds in such places. In addition, scats are easily found on roads and trails that wolves frequently travel. The scats found on these busier routes also provide samples whose general deposition date are more easily determined.

There are some difficulties in using scats to estimate wolf food preferences, however. Often wolf scats are not easily differentiated from those of domestic dogs or, in the United States, coyotes. Genetic testing of scats can be used to correctly categorize such scats, but it is often a prohibitively expensive procedure. Also, different food items are digested in different ways, and thus the resulting scats do not always indicate the same thing. For example, it has been shown that a wolf eating a certain amount of snowshoe hare would produce many more scats than would eating the same amount of moose. This is because, as a rule, a meal of 2 kg (2.2 lb) of hare has much more hair in proportion to meat than does the same mass of moose (the surface-to-body ratio of animals is higher for small animals vs. large ones). As another example, a pup's stomach full of crickets or grasshoppers may not be nutritionally equal to a stomach full of mice. Finally, remains of prey in scats do not always indicate the species of

No matter where wolves live, they rely mainly on large ungulates for food, and finding their carcasses, especially in winter, is fairly easy. However, wolves eat many other kinds of food that are less easily found and identified, and a complete assessment of wolf food habits includes analyses of wolf feces, called "scats".

animals that a wolf might kill. Wolves are great scavengers, to the point of having maggots turn up in scats, and thus scat analyses need to be interpreted with caution.

One additional method that has been used to help identify wolf diet on a large scale is isotope "tracers". Certain atomic isotopes are more common in certain food chains or systems throughout the world, and those isotopes can be detected in wolves. For instance, marine systems often have a different isotope ratio than do adjacent terrestrial systems, and the degree to which marine prey (e.g., scavenged seal carcasses or spawning salmon) are important to certain wolves could be identified.

Diet

Wolves are opportunistic foragers. This means they are experts at taking advantage of whatever circumstances they encounter to get something worthwhile to eat. The key, however, is getting something that is "worthwhile". Despite claims in the famous book and movie, *Never Cry Wolf*, wolves cannot make a living by just eating mice. I have no doubt that they can consume a large number of voles in the tundra or taiga when those species experience cyclic population highs and the whole ground surface seems to move with the scurrying of small rodents. But in the long run, it just costs wolves too much energy to catch enough mice to survive on. Because of the wolf's relatively large body size, and despite the inherent dangers in trying to catch and kill a moose, it is still easier and more efficient physiologically for a wolf to catch a moose than a moose's weight in rodents.

The kind of wild ungulate species that wolves catch and consume is directly related to geographic circumstances. Wolves will attempt to capture any large prey present in an area, though the frequency with which they do so may depend on the alternative prey available. Often, in any one area there is one large species that is both common and ubiquitous, and this is the one wolves consume most often. For example, in much of the boreal forest and taiga across Canada, northern Scandinavia, and Russia, moose are the only prey available and thus comprise the majority of wolf food. Similarly, caribou in the Western Hemisphere and reindeer in the Eastern Hemisphere are a predominant ungulate in the tundra that wolves specialize on. Still, wolves also kill roe deer, red deer, elk, and white-tailed deer where moose are common, and they kill musk oxen, Dall's sheep, and moose where caribou are common.

The list of ungulate species that wolves prey on is long and varied. In addition to the species just mentioned, Eurasian wolves from Norway to India, and from France to China also commonly kill wild boar, mouflon, European bison, saiga antelope, ibex, chamois, mountain goats, fallow deer, musk deer, sika deer, Mongolian gazelles, and blackbuck. There is no species of gazelle or horse that has not been killed by wolves, and even rare species such as bactrian camels in Mongolia and chiru in Tibet are not immune from wolf predation. In North America, wolves from Mexico north also kill mule deer, bison, mountain sheep, pronghorns, and mountain goats.

Throughout wolf range, many wild ungulates have been completely eliminated from the landscape by people and have been replaced by domestic ungulates. Not surprisingly, wolves easily developed a taste for these species, too, regardless of continent. Thus, horses, donkeys, cows, sheep, goats, pigs, llamas, and domestic yaks, reindeer and camels have all become wolf prey. Wolves also killed and sometimes consume domestic dogs, and undoubtedly domestic cats and rabbits, too.

Although wolves usually get most of their prey biomass in the form of ungulates, some other species are eaten, as well. In both North America and Eurasia, beavers are commonly consumed when they become most available. Usually this is in spring, when their winter food cache is exhausted and beavers begin foraging on land, or in the fall when yearling and 2-year-old beavers disperse from their streams and ponds to find new areas in which to settle. Hares of a variety of species are sometimes an important component of wolves' diets, too. Arctic hares are one of the few relatively common prey species in Canada's far north and are often hunted when musk oxen are hard to find. Snowshoe, blue, and mountain hares also are eaten commonly when their populations reach cyclic peaks. Recently, wolves were observed spending significant time at coastal streams where salmon aggregate to spawn. They can catch live fish at the rate of 20 per hour, and seem to eat just the heads before catching a new fish. Salmon are certainly a critical food item for brown bears in certain areas at specific times of the year, and this might be true for some wolves, too.

Other prey species probably are eaten opportunistically; that is, whenever it is relatively easy to catch them. Wolves probably don't go out of their way to catch mice and voles, marmots and woodchucks, ruffed and black grouse, or grasshoppers. But they show up fairly regularly in scats, especially during summer when snow cover is gone, as more species are active and available to wolves, and reproduction is at its highest. Bird eggs and nestlings are likely consumed when encountered, as well. Wolves may rely mainly on killing their own prey in many areas, but are also opportunistic scavengers that will readily feed on carcasses of animals that died of other causes.

Fruit-eating seems more common in Eurasia than in North America, although wolves do eat blueberries and raspberries in the latter. Wolves in Italy spend time in mature vineyards, and elsewhere in Europe they commonly eat cherries, berries, apples, pears, figs, and melons. In addition to calories from sugar, fruit may provide wolves with vitamins in summer. One additional plant "food" that often shows up in scats is grass. It probably is not nutritionally important to wolves, though it may provide some vitamins, and is suspected to act as a scour or inducement to vomit to get rid of intestinal parasites or long guard hairs that may impede digestion.

Finally, it is not uncommon to find that wolves visit or even frequent human refuse sites. Some of these sites provide food in the form of remains of domestic animals (offal) and the leavings of human meals of meat, fruit and vegetables, and even pasta. Often wolves feeding at dumps ingest non-food garbage, too, including human hair, plastic, tin foil, cigarettes, matches, and glass. Many wolves feed at these sites because natural prey are scarce, and domestic livestock is well-tended and therefore scarce as well.

Hunting and Killing
Behavior

Endurance, aggressiveness, and experience are probably the traits that make a wolf a good hunter. They may travel 40-50 km (20-30 mi) between kills, potentially in a single night, continuously searching for prey. Wolves can run 60 km/hr (35 mi/hr) for several minutes, and can continue to run fast for more than 20 minutes while on the trail of prey. When they find it, it is most often bigger than the wolf, sometimes 10 times bigger and more. It must take a combination of boldness and confidence for a wolf to tackle a moose or bison, and a lot of experience to know when to abandon the attempt. Finally, an intimate knowledge of the distribution of food makes hunting more efficient. In a winter that is hard for wolves this may mean the difference between living and starving. On Isle Royale, for instance, a hunting pack traveled straight across the island one winter to find a surviving moose that had been wounded 6 weeks before.

The first part of a hunt obviously involves finding the prey, which requires significant travel. Most prey animals are mobile and relatively scarce, so the distances wolves travel is necessarily large. Indeed, in winter wolves have spent anywhere from 28-50% of their time traveling. Prey animals are detected by sight and/or smell, most often in chance encounters, but probably in areas where the wolves have had some previous success. In snowy winters, wolves often hunt in single file to save energy, but they

Wolves on the tundra of Ellesmere Island, northern Canada, hunt groups of musk oxen, with the hope of separating out one of the young, relatively defenceless ones. Many of the animals that wolves hunt are formidable opponents, and most have strategies to reduce the chances that they will be preyed on by wolves.

Dall's sheep living in northwest Canada and Alaska use precipitous mountain slopes to escape attacks, and relatively few are surprised and killed by wolves. Where other types of prey animals are scarce, however, individual wolves must learn how to hunt these sheep successfully, most often by climbing above them and chasing them downhill.

have been seen to fan out under certain circumstances, presumably to increase chances of finding prey. Many more prey animals are found than are actually attacked or killed because a large number of animals that are targeted either outrun or are able to fight off their attackers. The hunting success rate for moose, for example, may be only 8% or so; this means only 1 in 12 or 13 moose encountered is actually killed by hunting wolves.

Unless the initial contact with prey animals results in the prey running off immediately, wolves will attempt to stalk an animal to get as close as possible. They seem to remain restrained but excited, and have been seen to make use of uneven terrain to get close. If the prey animal initially runs, or when stalking wolves are detected and the prey runs off, wolves immediately give chase. If the prey is small and alone, such as a hare, deer, or caribou calf, wolves seem to try to catch it as quickly as they can because it is likely that the wolf can easily kill such animals. Wolves will run along with large prey animals for a bit, seemingly to evaluate which one might be most vulnerable and easiest to kill. This testing seems to work; large prey animals killed by wolves are not a random sample of the population, but seem to have characteristics such as inexperience or injury that destine them to be killed. Sometimes when prey animals detect wolves, they actually move toward the wolves or stand their ground. This behavior is most common of larger prey such as moose, bison, and musk ox. In these cases, wolves approach the prey animals but wait until the animal runs before getting close enough to grab onto it. If they prey stands it's ground for a long enough time, the wolves usually give up and move on.

It seems logical that a pair of wolves would be more efficient hunters than would a single wolf. A pair could maneuver better, keep up with running prey, and one wolf could distract the prey animal while another one attacks. We know that single wolves can kill prey animals of all sizes, just as pairs and larger groups do, but we don't know how efficient they are in such hunts. What we do know is that, despite the relatively large size of packs, pairs of wolves are more efficient (more meat per individual) in killing prey animals than are larger packs. In other words, there is no data supporting the notion that wolves in big packs are better killers because of higher numbers. Lions are known to hunt strategically and cooperatively, i.e., chasing into ambush, heading off fleeing prey, or taking turns chasing prey, so why not wolves? Wolves do seem to hunt Dall's sheep successfully only when they can get above them and thus chase them downhill; such sheep can easily outrun wolves going uphill. And when involved in long, strung-out chases on open ground (such as caribou on the tundra), trailing wolves do seem to cut corners and thus get closer to prey animals. But it turns out that wolves are rarely observed to actually cooperate much when chasing prey. This may be because wolves don't really stay long in packs, and with relatively high mortality rates, even pairs aren't together for many years. It may be, too, that long distance chases are just not very conducive to tactical or strategic hunts, and wolves seem to survive just fine without such cooperation.

There does seem to be some cooperation, or at least diversified assistance, when wolves actually grab onto a prey animal and kill it. The teeth of wolves are adapted to stab, hold on to, and then pull at prey to try and drag it down. This grabbing action also serves to rip and cut hide and muscle, disabling and causing extensive bleeding of prey animals. As mentioned before, a single wolf can kill large prey by itself, but having some pack members distract the prey while others lunge at it seems useful. A characteristic of some packs killing moose is that a single wolf will grab on to the very large nose and pull at it with all its might. This seems to hold the moose rather still (like a ring in a bull's nose or peg in a camel's nose) and its pack mates then grab onto the hindquarters and start cutting and tearing. The death of an ungulate by wolves is not instantaneous, but may be as quick as the strangulation hold of a lion. Loss of blood likely causes a prey animal to go into shock in a short period of time, and soon after leads to death.

Kill Rates

Since the hunting of large animals by wolves is a risky business, it should not be surprising that capture success rates of wolves are generally low. Most data has been gathered in winter when vulnerability of prey is at its highest, and thus the success rates are probably higher then than they are in the summer. Still, recorded success has averaged only 25% (range = 10-49%) when hunting groups of moose, herds of caribou, Dall's sheep, bison, and elk (wolves chase a herd averaging 1-18 animals and 1 is successfully killed) and only 14% (range = 1-56%) when considering all available individuals (also including white-tailed deer). There are no consistent species-specific success rates, probably because success varies with time of day, weather, terrain, predator experience, prey species, number, sex, age, associates, vulnerability, etc.

Even with this relatively low success rate, wolves still must kill enough to maintain themselves. The actual number of prey killed by a pack each year is difficult to estimate because kills are hard to find during the summer, and food habits vary seasonally. By taking these and other factors into account, however, it has been estimated in different studies that an individual wolf might be responsible, depending on the area, for consuming 15-19 adult white-tailed deer, or 16 adult cow caribou, or 4 adult and 5 calf moose each year.

On rare occasions, however, wolves do what is termed "surplus killing". This behavior is said to occur when wolves kill repeatedly over a short period of time and eat little or none of the carcasses. This only usually occurs when prey are both very abundant and highly vulnerable. When it does happen, it often involves either newborn ungulates, such as caribou calves in a calving ground, or older ungulates in a herd that become immobilized by very deep snow. It does occur more often with herds of domestic animals, as they lack normal defenses against wolf predation.

Prey Selectivity

Wolves probably consider trying to catch and kill every prey animal that they encounter. But more often than not, they seem to pass by many individuals without so much as a turned head or a directed step. In many situations where more than one species of prey is present, wolves end up killing a disproportionate number of one vs. the other(s). Even where only a single species is hunted, wolves do not kill a random sample of individuals, but rather they more often kill certain sex- and age-classes. So what causes wolves to kill what they kill?

It seems clear that selection of prey by wolves relates directly to prey vulnerability. Wolves seem to balance capture efficiency and profitability with the risk of making a particular kill. As wolves travel around their territory, they constantly locate and test prey under a variety of circumstances. In doing this, they gain information and experience concerning prey vulnerability. Those prey animals that are the easiest and safest to kill are the ones most commonly killed by wolves.

The ease of capture clearly changes with a variety of characteristics and circumstances, some of which seem obvious and others that are more subtle. Wolves kill fawns or calves of any age, but seem to kill newborn ones more often that one would expect if they killed prey randomly. These juvenile animals are not as fast and certainly not as experienced as older animals, thus are easier to catch. They are also smaller than others of their species, and thus safer for wolves to catch. It also turns out that fawns or calves born after their mothers have experienced a severe and condition-depleting winter, are born smaller than normal. Throughout their lives they appear not to grow as large as normal and as a result seem to be killed by wolves relatively more often than larger animals of similar ages.

Prey animals that might be considered elderly for their species are also killed more often than healthy adults. Although there is good reason — experience — that they have lived to a ripe old age,

Bull moose in their prime (i.e., 5-8 years old) are extremely difficult for wolves to kill.
Most often, calf moose and very old moose are the ones that wolves end up being able to catch.

elderly prey are likely to be in poorer condition for a variety of reasons, and thus easier to catch. They may be in poorer condition because their teeth are worn or diseased, and thus they cannot process food as well as younger animals. Many old moose are arthritic and they probably can't run as fast or confidently as younger animals. They may also be generally more diseased, perhaps by parasitic tapeworms or some other parasite, and thus less able to defend themselves.

Animals that show some abnormal behavior might stand out in a herd and be a focus of hunting wolves. For example, an elk or red deer that has become lame due to an arthritic knee joint might be a step slower, show an awkward gait going uphill, or not be able to turn as well as a healthy animal. Wolves seem to home in on such behavior and pursue such animals disproportionately more often than they do others.

Species abundance clearly has some affect on prey selection where multiple prey species occur, especially where one species is quite rare. Wolves that I watched from an airplane in northcentral Minnesota always hunted white-tailed deer. Still, a few moose did live in the area, and the only hunt of a moose that I saw did not last long. A pack of seven wolves encountered a cow moose and her calf one winter and immediately gave chase. While the wolves quickly closed the 100-m gap between them and the moose, the cow trotted along making sure the calf was in front of her. When the lead wolf got very close, she first kicked out a hind foot, and then turned around to face the wolf. At this, the wolf slid to a quick stop 3 m from the moose, looked up for a second, and immediately abandoned the hunt. It seemed clear that the wolf had not encountered a "deer" five times the normal size before and was completely at a loss as to how to proceed.

The ease of killing certain species vs. others also is evident in records of wolf kills. In general, where the two prey species are both moderately abundant, wolves seem to prefer preying on deer or caribou or elk vs. moose, and moose vs. mountain sheep

or goats or bison. Bigger prey are probably harder and more dangerous to kill than smaller prey, and prey living in precipitous landscapes are also relatively less easy to capture.

Changes in species abundance over time also affects prey selection. Wolves in northeastern Minnesota almost always hunted white-tailed deer until the population fell so low that moose seemed as or more abundant than deer. Some packs of wolves significantly augmented their diet of deer with moose, but others completely shifted their hunting behavior and selected moose almost exclusively.

Feeding

There is a reason for the expression, "wolfing down" your food; wolves are voracious eaters. An adult beaver, a deer fawn, or a yearling caribou can all be consumed by a pack of wolves within an hour or two. Even a 150-kg (330-lb) moose calf can be eaten so quickly and completely that nothing but a mat of hair remains at the kill site. For larger prey, there may be something left after a couple of hours, but its not for lack of trying on the part of the wolves. One of the reasons wolves eat fresh kills so quickly is because they are the easiest for scavengers to consume as well. Any leftovers from the wolves' first feeding that is not covered with thick hide, or in winter becomes frozen, is available for smaller animals to take. The other reason for the speed of feeding is probably that the wolves are so hungry. Often it has been several days to more than a week since the last meal, and the best physiological strategy may be to eat as much as you can as fast as you can.

Usually the most dominant, "alpha" male and female wolves have, or take, feeding priority. This may be because they are often the breeding adults and thus parents to the rest of the pack, but also because they usually do most of the actual killing. Sometimes they rest just after making a kill, however, and other pack members begin feeding first. These first feeders may finish a continuous feeding bout in anywhere from 15 minutes to an hour, depending on the pack size and social relationship of pack members.

The first parts of a carcass that are consumed are often the large internal organs (lungs, heart, and liver). The large rumen (stomach) is usually torn during its removal and the vegetal contents spilled. The wolves have no interest in rumen contents, but they do eat the stomach and intestine, along with smaller organs such as the kidneys and spleen. Concurrently, some wolves may be eating skin, back muscles, leg muscles, and meat from the ribs. Skulls are gnawed and for smaller animals are broken open so that the brains can be eaten, as well.

Well-fed wolves may have stomachs so distended that they can only sleep on their side, not curled up. This is not surprising, given that they may have consumed almost 25% of their body weight (see Chapter 2 – Morphology). They may rest for 5 or 6 hours before feeding again, eating whatever meat and skin they can find, as well as crunching up bones to get marrow as well as the calcium and phosphorous in the bones themselves.

Based on detailed records of kills made by numerous packs throughout North America, estimated average daily food consumption was 5.4 kg (12 lb) of food per wolf per day. This varied from 2.3-11.2 kg (5-24 lb) per wolf per day in different study areas, probably reflecting the different kill rates by packs of different sizes. These values compare favorably with the calculated minimum daily requirement (3.3 kg [7.2 lb] per wolf per day) based on metabolic rates, activity rates, body size, and food type. The higher values described for wild wolves likely represent very high kill rates, and thus the amount of food available to be eaten by the wolves rather than that actually consumed by them. What the wolves didn't eat perhaps ended up in one of two places. Some may have been frozen and not consumed by wolves until it thawed the next spring. Much, however, likely ended up in the stomachs of numerous scavengers that would certainly be attracted to such an abundant food source.

The degree to which a carcass is completely utilized depends on the wolves' nutritional status at the time of the kill, the size of the kill, and the number of wolves feeding on it. On average, winter weather conditions may play a significant role in carcass use because it can affect ungulate vulnerability to wolf predation (see Chapter 9 – Species Interactions). For example, wolves I studied in Minnesota seemed to feed well but not excessively on deer carcasses in 3 winters when snow depths were average and kill rates were moderately high. Also, the wolves rarely revisited old carcasses in those winters. When snow is greater than about 40 cm (16 in) deep it is difficult for deer to run and, consequently, easier for wolves to catch them. In contrast, wolves had a hard time catching deer in 3 other winters when snow was shallow. Carcasses were consumed completely, and wolves had a high carcass revisitation rate all winter.

When wolves are full and can't eat any more, they cache food. Caches may contain a few chunks of regurgitated meat, or a whole hare or caribou calf. Caching usually happens in the spring or summer when wolves hunt singly or in pairs, and thus any kill they make likely has more meat on it than can be eaten in one sitting. Caching certainly serves to protect food from scavengers, and it also provides future meals if nobody else raids the cache. Sometimes wolves cache food immediately after feeding. Wolves have been observed to travel up to 5 km from kills to cache food, and have made as many as six caches after feeding.

Some species make a living by paying attention to where wolves go and what they kill. There are a variety of scavengers that depend, to some extent, on wolves, including beetles, and all of them reduce the amount of food that is available for wolves to eat. The amount of any kill that is lost to scavengers is dependent on the size of the pack that feeds at the kill. As expected, larger packs eat kills more rapidly and there is less opportunity for scavengers to feed. As a result, a lone wolf might lose two-thirds of a moose carcass to scavengers, a pair of wolf about half a moose, but a pack of 10 wolves might lose only about 10% or none at all.

Species Interactions:
How do other Animals Interact with Wolves?

Prey Relationships

It is obvious from food habits studies (see Chapter 8 – Food) that many species of animals, and particularly the ungulates or hoofed mammals, are wolf prey. But how is it that over thousands of years, there seems to be some kind of balance among these species, and there always seem enough prey around for wolves to eat? Prey animals must be doing something right to avoid being wiped out by wolves, and the environment that they are adapted to, and even thrive in, must somehow mitigate the effects of wolves.

Prey Defenses

All species possess a combination of physical traits and behaviors that provide major survival benefits related to predation by wolves or other predators. Sheer size may help the largest ungulates such as bison, moose, horses, musk oxen, elk, and even wild boar, especially when combined with aggressive behavior. These species certainly do run to escape wolves, but often stand and fight, and in doing so end up winning more often than not. Antlers and horns, as well as well-aimed hooves, are defensive weapons that, in the case of moose, musk ox, and deer, have been known to kill attacking wolves. Some species do not depend on combative defense for survival, but rather use their ability to run quickly and with agility to escape wolf predation. Gazelles and pronghorns on the open plains are among the swiftest of all mammals. The speed and leaping ability of many deer allow them to escape through forest cover where few other species can keep pace. The newborn young of some species have cryptic coloration which allows them to hide more easily from predators; they also lack distinctive scents that might attract wolves to their location.

Another anti-predator strategy used by many ungulates is to concentrate their births during a short period of time, a phenomenon called birth synchrony. Presumably, when highly vulnerable young are all born at once, predators such as wolves are "swamped" with prey and only have time to find and kill a limited number of calves or fawns; in the mean time, the other newborns grow quickly and are then less vulnerable to predation. As an alternative to hiding for the first several days of life, calves of some species such as moose follow their mother closely immediately after birth and can nearly even keep up with a running mother. This, in combination with defensive behavior by mothers, gives the calves enough of a head start that, if they survive the first couple of weeks, they can run as fast as any adult.

The level of vigilance by prey is affected by several factors. Large-bodied species are generally more observant of large predators than are smaller species, and individual animals in large herds are less watchful than when they are in smaller groups and thus have fewer "eyes" scanning for predators. Similarly, individuals in the middle of herds are less wary than those at the periphery. Mothers with newborn young are definitely more attentive and on guard than other individuals, presumably because their investment is so high and their offspring are so vulnerable. Ungulates in thick cover also seem to be more vigilant than those in open areas because it is so much easier for predators to approach closely where vegetation is dense. Also, prey animals seem to increase their watchfulness after wolves have hunted in an area.

Some ungulates such as deer and sheep may vocalize when a predator is seen and thereby alert their neighbors. White-tailed deer raise their conspicuous white tail after detecting and fleeing a predator, presumably to let the predator (and other deer?) know that they have been seen and therefore that it is useless to follow. Species that are vulnerable to wolf predation when running have group defensive behaviors that are effective deterrents. For example, musk oxen form a defensive line or ring to shield their young when a predator is detected. They press their rumps together in front of their young, the young crowd toward them, and the wall or ring of sharp horns that faces the wolves is formidable. Herding, in general, seems to be a defensive mechanism for many species. At least during some seasons, antelope, elk, wild boar, and musk oxen all travel in herds. Presumably this behavior results in higher detection rates of

predators, a dilution of risk of getting killed, greater physical defense, and increased confusion for predators.

In addition to making best use of seasonal food resources, migratory ungulates often have reduced their risk of predation by making it more difficult for predators to find them. Some wide-ranging species that are not considered migratory also seem to gain benefits by moving nomadically around their range, sometimes covering vast distances. One herd of bison moved greater than 80 km (50 mi) within 24 hours after wolves killed a calf in their herd.

Theoretically, prey animals could maximize the time wolves spending searching for prey by spacing themselves out, thus minimizing the chances that wolves would find them. "Spacing

away" from wolves is often a more practical tactic, best exemplified by migratory caribou in the Canadian Arctic. The distant location of their calving grounds end up being far enough from denning wolves that it is not very practical for the wolves to make the trip to hunt them. Some woodland caribou give birth in isolated locations not usually occupied by caribou and thus not frequently visited by wolves. Deer in parts of Minnesota and on Vancouver Island in Canada seem to "space away" from wolves by disproportionately inhabiting the buffer areas between wolf pack territories. Wolves spend less time in these areas because of the increased chance of a fatal encounter with a neighboring pack (see Chapter 5 – Land Use), and thus zones are relatively safer from predation than are the interiors of territories.

Many species make use of escape features in the environment to avoid predation. By running into water, long-legged ungulates, aside from making wolves swim, may give shorter-legged wolves less leverage. Wolves rarely if ever go into the water to catch beavers, but instead wait for them to come out on land. On the other hand, a swimming wolf has been observed killing a swimming deer. Steep terrain clearly plays a role in the survival of sheep and goats; these species are almost defenseless on level ground, but once on rocks and cliffs it is extremely difficult for wolves to kill them. Some species, especially when giving birth, use islands, shorelines, peninsulas, and elevated sites in forest as a means to reduce the chances of a predator sneaking up on them, and wild boars use burrows to avoid predators.

Influences of Predation

A major concern regarding wolf populations is their effect on prey populations. For example, will moose or deer numbers increase if wolf numbers are reduced? Conversely, will there be fewer prey animals if wolves are reintroduced into an area? One would like to believe that, given all the effort that has gone into studying wolf-prey relationships, there is some predictability to the answers to these questions. It turns out, however, that this is not a simple laboratory interaction. There are some good general conclusions that can be drawn, but specific situations are all a bit different.

The effect of predation on a prey population depends, first of all, on the rates at which wolves kill their prey. Predation rates do vary quite a bit (see Chapter 8 – Food), but on a population-by-population basis, per capita kill rates (kg/wolf/day) are fairly consistent because wolves need a certain amount of food to eat. Second, the total amount or number of prey killed in an area depends on how many wolves there are. The question, then, is whether or not the prey population can sustain the rate of mortality from wolves. The answer depends on two things: 1) what the density of prey is and 2) how "fast" do they reproduce. The rate at which prey reproduce is a function of their food resources. Regardless of food abundance for prey, there has to be enough prey around to produce enough offspring such that production is at least equal to the number killed by wolves and other predators. When neither wolf nor prey (i.e., ungulate) populations are in the middle of some major change or fluctuation, and thus somewhat balanced, there usually seems to be about 125-200 deer-sized ungulates (or 40-60 elk, or 20-30 moose) for every wolf.

In addition to the effects of wolves, prey population numbers also have natural fluctuations in response to the vegetation (their food source) and weather. Relatively abundant food means that reproduction and survival is higher because animals are in better condition; this generally leads to population growth. On the other hand, a population might be in decline if food availability is poor. Exceptionally harsh winter weather can lead to major population declines because of starvation and increase susceptibility to predation, and a mild winter make allow otherwise stressed animals to survive.

Another confounding factor in the wolf-prey relationship is the abundance of other predators. Brown bears in particular, but also black bears, can be major predators on calves/fawns, depending on the density of both bears and prey. The added mortality due to bears in a wolf-ungulate system may lead to a situation where the prey population is held at a much lower level than it would be if only bears or only wolves were present. The situation becomes even more complex when there are multiple species of prey in a system. In some places, caribou numbers are held down by wolf predation because a large moose population that lives in the same area supports a relatively high number of wolves. The wolves just feed on caribou when its easy to do so. Without moose, low caribou numbers ordinarily translate into low wolf numbers, but not in this scenario. And things get more complex when the prey species is migratory. This means that in a given area, the prey available to wolves fluctuates greatly throughout the year, and may not be very predictable to wolves or biologists at any one time.

Finally, almost every wolf-ungulate system in the world is affected by humans. Humans may hunt prey for meat or hides, and may kill wolves and other predators for their pelts or just to keep their numbers down so that there is more prey for the humans. This added mortality factor is not very predictable in most cases, yet can have major consequences to the predator prey system.

In sum, it's the vegetation that sets the limit as to how many ungulates might be in an area. When wolf predation is the major cause of ungulate mortality, vegetation, wolves, and weather work in consort to regulate the ungulate population. In some years the wolves gain a bit, in other years the ungulates do. Over time, it all evens out if no other outside factors shift the dynamic balance.

Predators and Competitors

There are several other categories of animals beside prey with which wolves interact. If wolves don't eat them, then either wolves compete for food with them, are killed and sometimes eaten by them, or have no direct interaction with them at all. Because of the hemispheric distribution of wolves, they interact with a wide variety of species under myriad circumstances.

Wolves and brown bears live together in many parts of the world, and they sometimes encounter each other at the remains of prey. A female with cubs may not have killed this moose in Denali Park, Alaska, but the scavenged prize is worth defending because the much needed protein it contains is difficult to come by.

Most of the non-prey species that interact with wolves are mammalian or avian carnivores and scavengers. In the wolf's role as predator and scavenger, there is ample opportunity to have overlapping food preferences with these other species. Thus, the differential utilization of food resources constitutes the primary relationship between wolves and non-prey species. This competition for food generally takes place in two ways. First, species specialize on different kinds of prey in an area, though their overall diet may overlap somewhat. And second, there occasionally are confrontations between species trying to consume the same kinds of food. Both of these kinds of competition occur with wolves, and the degree to which each is prominent depends on the competing species.

Bears

Brown bears once had a geographic range only slightly less southerly than wolves. Although the current range of brown bears is much smaller than that of wolves, they do live together (are sympatric) in many parts of the world. Brown bears are omnivorous – they eat substantial plant and insect food in addition to meat – but they are very effective carnivores, as well. Most of the wolf-brown bear interactions take place at kill sites, mostly those of wolves where the bears are scavenging, but also those of bears where wolves are scavenging. Usually, bears win these encounters, and because wolves make more kills than bears, bears end up with a net gain of food. Wolf-bear encounters at kills may be brief, but some have lasted several hours with feeding and attacking going on continuously. Bear also investigate wolf dens in the spring and sometimes kill pups.

Wolves and North American black bears also have overlapping ranges and directly interact with each other. Some interactions occur at kills made by wolves, and wolves usually win these encounters. Interestingly, wolves also appear to seek out black bears in dens and on at least six reported occasions have killed

the bears. Wolf interactions with polar bears are rare, but wolves have been observed to kill and consume a polar bear cub, and to contest a caribou kill near a polar bear den.

Big Cats

Wolves and cougars, or mountain lions, in North America both live primarily on ungulates, but the two species hunt in very different ways. Unlike wolves that chase down prey, cougars hunt by stealth, stalking and ambushing prey animals in relatively thick cover and rough terrain. To some extent these different techniques may provide some separation between the species. In winters when snow forces most ungulates into mountainous river valleys, however, the two species do interact over kills and each has been observed to kill the other.

Historically, the distribution of tigers in Asia significantly overlapped that of wolves, but now does so in a major way only in the Russian Far East (a few wolves and tigers may have overlapping ranges in India). Both are known to eat the same species of prey, but their direct interactions are rarely reported. Biologists interpreting wolf tracks in tiger range did report that when the wolves came upon fresh tiger tracks, they immediately turned around and headed the other direction. Wolves have been displaced from kills by tigers, and one or two wolves have been reported killed by tigers.

Wolves do occur in areas of Asia inhabited by snow leopards and common leopards, but no records of interactions with these species exist. Also, wolves historically lived in the same areas of Mexico as jaguars, but there are no good records of interactions there, either.

Other Canids

The most studied relationship between wolves and another canid species is that with coyotes in North America. In general, wolf and coyote numbers seem to be inversely related to one another, indicating that wolves displace or kill coyotes in many instances. Coyotes certainly try to scavenge carcasses of prey killed by wolves, and that is where they are most often killed. In many places, however, coyotes are able to live and successfully breed at the boundaries of wolf territories where the chances of encountering packs are less. On rare occasions coyotes successfully chase wolves; usually these have been near coyote dens sites and where their numbers have equaled or exceeded those of the wolves.

Wolves kill and sometimes eat red foxes. Again, this most often occurs when foxes are attempting to scavenge from wolf kills, which can be an important source of winter food for them. In the long run, however, it may be better for foxes to live where wolves do. Coyotes are actually stronger direct competitors with foxes than are wolves, so when wolves reduce the coyote population, red fox populations may actually increase in comparison to when only coyotes are present. Wolf interactions with Arctic foxes are probably similar to those with red foxes, but none have been reported in the scientific literature.

Dholes, also known as Asiatic wild dogs or whistling dogs, are pack canids that behave like wolves elsewhere in wolf range. In India, however, some wolves behave more like coyotes, with family groups rarely including more than a pair of adults and their pups of the year. Similar to the wolf-coyote interactions in North America, dhole packs apparently can displace wolf pairs from prime habitat and those wolves subsist in less optimal circumstances. In Asia, interactions of wolves with golden jackals may be similar to those of wolves with coyotes when jackals are the next largest canid species in the area. In Poland, raccoon dogs are reported to be killed and even consumed by wolves.

Ravens and Other Species

Ravens in North America seem to interact with wolves more than any other non-prey species. In particular, ravens focus their activity at wolf kill sites, where over time flocks of them may be able to remove as much as 10-66% of the meat from a kill, depending on the number of wolves at the kill site. Raven are sometimes caught and killed by wolves while scavenging, but raven welfare may depend heavily on such carcasses and the risk is clearly worth the effort. In Yellowstone National Park in the U.S., ravens follow wolves while they are hunting. They do not follow coyotes, or elk, and do not frequent areas that lack wolves. This is rewarding behavior; during one winter, ravens discovered 100% of the ungulates wolves killed there.

Eurasian lynx and wolves are sympatric across much of their range, and they often feed on the same species, usually roe deer. Some food habits studies suggest that where wolves are plentiful, lynx eat relatively less roe deer and more hares, but no observations of interactions have been reported. Interactions between wolverines and wolves often have resulted in the death of the wolverine.

Although most of the reported incidences have not been at kill sites, wolverines depend on carcasses for food in winter and it is likely that they visit wolf kills often. Wolves and striped hyenas are sympatric in southern Asia, but interactions between them have only been reported from garbage dumps.

Single wolves generally made way for a larger hyena, but a pack of wolves could displace one. In North America, wolves have killed river otters, skunks, American martens, badgers, and golden eagles. A short-toed eagle was killed in India when apparently attempting to catch pups feeding at a carcass. Overall, the coexistence of wolves and other non-prey species varies from benign to deadly. This largely depends on the degree to which there are conflicts over food, the relative size of each species, the taxonomic relationships, and thus the relative similarity of the species. Our understanding of many of these relationships is very limited, and for others essentially unknown (e.g., wolves and striped hyenas), but all are fascinating to contemplate.

Humans:
How do Humans and Wolves Interact?

Human Attitudes

Contemporary human attitudes and values concerning wolves run a gamut from adoration to repugnancy. But one has to wonder why it is that some people believe wolves are the ultimate symbol of wilderness and environmental completeness, while others are convinced that wolves represent nature out of control, wreaking havoc on mankind.

Many negative feelings are clearly reactions to the practical problems that humans must face when living with wolves. Most farmers would be angered to discover a wolf standing over a dead, pregnant ewe. But just as many urbanites, few of which have ever walked in wolf country, would be enraged when viewing a videotape of wolves being shot so that an elk population could increase for hunters. As one might guess, many of the thoughts and outlooks that people have today result from a mix of historical perceptions that have perpetuated throughout many cultures, along with new values learned during their lifetimes. As a result, there are probably as many negative and positive values associated with wolves today as there ever have been.

So what is it about the interactions of humans and wolves that have caused this disparity? Perhaps the best way to begin to understand this relationship is to identify how wolves directly threaten or otherwise react to humans, and to describe how and why humans deal with wolves in the ways they do. We should then review the myths and legends concerning wolves in order to assess how they may have come about, how truthful they might be, and how they influence current day attitudes towards wolves. From this, new contemporary views of wolves may be more understandable.

Wolf Reactions to Humans

Wolves Killing Humans

How wolves behave with humans seems to depend to a large extent on their previous experience and the current conditions. Wolves without any experience of humans often approach them with curiosity, and no doubt with some uncertainty as to whether or not humans might be prey. Wolves that attack people might be doing so for defensive purposes, for instance when pups are vulnerable or they perceived themselves to be in danger that they cannot flee from. In some instances when food is scarce or children are unprotected and far from other people, it appears that wolves kill humans, too.

It also would seem to make sense that an animal that can kill a moose should be considered a threat to human safety. In Europe and Asia, there are historical records of wolf attacks on humans, but many appear to involve tame wolves, wolf-dog hybrids, or rabid wolves. By reviewing church and court records, government correspondence, state archives, and the like from the 15th to 20th centuries, researchers have identified wolves killing humans in Estonia, Northern Italy, Poland, Finland, Sweden, and Russia. In Italy, most of those killed were children, especially in rural areas; most adults were killed near villages or towns. In Russia, and other places, it was suggested that many incidents occurred during and after fights or wars when wolves became accustomed to feeding on corpses. In some instances the killing could be blamed on wolves that had been raised in captivity and then released. In general, wolf attacks in Europe and northern Asia seem quite rare and then occur mostly under special circumstances. More recently, compelling evidence of attacks by healthy wolves comes from India. Within the past 10-20 years,

For some people, wolves represent a direct threat to their livelihood; for others they are the ultimate symbol of wildness.

reports of wolves carrying away and eating small children, termed "child-lifting", have been documented by several researchers. In once instance a single wolf apparently killed or injured 76 children over a 7-month period in a rural, poverty-stricken area where wild prey animals were scarce and unattended children outnumbered unguarded livestock.

In contrast to those in Eurasia, wolves in North America seem to have a much-reduced propensity to attack humans. Inuit and American Indian cultures had regular interactions with wolves, and in some cases suffered killings by wolves, yet did not regard them as dangerous. Wolves did not attack early North American explorers and trappers either, though many observers familiar with stories from Europe were amazed at this. There have been recent cases of wolves acting aggressively toward humans in Ontario and British Columbia, Canada, and in Alaska. Some of these have resulted in injury, but most seem to represent "threats, defensive reactions, or some kind of non-predatory interaction." The only other reported incidences in North America appear to involve rabid wolves but, again, they seem to be very rare.

Other Wolf Reactions to Humans

As noted previously, the reactions of wolves to human behaviors, activities, and developments seem to depend on their experience. Where wolves have had little contact with people, or where they are accustomed to humans providing food for them, they show little fear. Prior to the advent of rifles that could injure or kill them from a distance, or vehicles that could chase them, wolves on the open grasslands seemed relatively indifferent to humans. This behavior is unlike that of wolves in forested areas, where they may have been more wary and secretive because they cannot see as far, and thus have to be more vigilant than steppe or grassland wolves.

Wolves, like many other animals, become conditioned to activities in their environment. Wolves, or their survivors, soon learn to avoid those that are harmful or lethal. For example, airplanes are not inherently dangerous to wolves, but those in northern Minnesota soon learned to run for cover when a plane approached because when there was a bounty for wolves, pilots or their passengers routinely shot wolves from the air. Scientists first began studying wolves just as the bounty and aerial shooting ended in Minnesota, and it took about a wolf generation or so before wolves became indifferent to airplanes. Now they usually do not even raise their heads when a biologist flies overhead at low altitude.

The reason why some people believe that wolves in North America are wilderness animals is not because they require wilderness, but because that is the only place that they have remained after persecution by humans. Indeed, parts of Europe are among the best of places to remind us that wolves can live among humans, even to the extent of foraging in the outskirts of or passing through villages, towns, and cities. Usually, however, such activity occurs at night when the chances of direct contact with humans is low.

Wolves have learned that where wolves are not specifically protected, many encounters with humans are not positive, so they avoid places and times when human activity is high. Where they are protected, however, they may be seen and even observed for long periods of time, acting as they do when no humans are around. Wolves den near logging activities, pass near hikers, and reside on military bases where they encounter all sorts of human activities. Wolves travel on roads and trails routinely, although they also represent some small danger because of speeding vehicles. In the U.S., the density of roads has been used as an index of wolf habitat suitability, not only because a low density means a low collision rate, but, more importantly, because high road density means more encounters with people, especially those who use roads as access to hunting and trapping areas, and thus have a proclivity to kill wolves.

Wolves have been killed by humans for thousands of years, sometimes for their pelts, sometimes for food, and often for protection of game or livestock. Aboriginal North Americans killed wolf pups in dens when numbers seemed high relative to the availability of game species. Throughout the world wolves have been and continue to be poisoned, trapped, snared, and shot to reduce or eliminate their depredations on cattle, sheep, horses, goats, and camels. There is still an international market for wolf pelts, as well, and this can be a substantial source of income for some people.

Human Reactions to Wolves

Humans Killing Wolves

People kill wolves for a variety of reasons. Understandably, wolves have been killed in self-defense, but probably more often they have been killed in defense of property. They have been killed for their use as a product, for sport, and to increase the opportunities for humans to hunt game animals, as well. As a result, wolves have been trapped, using steel-jawed foothold traps, corral or cage traps, pitfall traps, and deadfalls. Wolves have been snared, poisoned, shot, and hunted with eagles and hounds. Some Eskimos coiled sharpened willow sticks or strips of baleen in frozen tallow balls; after wolves ate the balls, the tallow would melt and the coils would unwind and pierce their stomachs. There seems no end to the ways in which humans kill wolves, and the justifications for such killing are almost as varied.

Humans and wolves have always competed for ungulate prey. Logically, to some, any deer that wolves killed (and they kill many deer each year; see Chapter 8) was one less available to a hungry hunter and his or her family. The fewer wolves there were, the more opportunities there should have been to kill a deer. Thus, wolves were speared or shot, and wolf dens were occasionally raided to kill pups to keep the wolf population "under control". Prehistorically, however, the effect of these human activities on the wolf population was not overwhelming.

It was not until human populations became large enough, and the numbers of wild ungulates low enough and therefore valuable enough, that humans turned their attention to trying to completely eliminate wolves as competitors. Some human cultures became very good at this. For example, wolves were completely gone from the British Isles over 400 years ago. In addition, wolves were even eliminated from Yellowstone National Park in the U.S. in the early 20th century to assure that the resident game populations would be able to thrive.

The wolf-game animal issue still is important and has become especially contentious where wolf reintroduction has been proposed. After decades of being able to hunt big game in wolf-free environments, hunters continually question scientists as to the effect of reintroducing wolves to an area and, more specifically, how much it will reduce the legal harvest of game by hunters. Where wolves are common, they often are legally harvested (such that their populations will remain viable) in order have sustainable hunting by humans of large ungulates. As part of intensive management plans for some northern predator-prey systems, wolf packs are purposefully targeted for elimination by government agencies. Theoretically, bad weather, high predator numbers, and/or over-harvest by humans can drive game populations to low levels. Even though the game species could perhaps out-reproduce wolves if given the chance, they apparently cannot do so when numerous wolves and bears, together, are preying on them. The temporary "control" of wolves sometimes seems to result in higher levels of sustainable use of both predator and prey. This may done with participation of the public, but more often is carried out by government officials using snares, or even helicopters and radio telemetry, to increase efficiency.

Wolves also have been and are killed because wolf fur has always been an important wolf product. It is used for coats, hats, pants, and trim, and sometimes for blankets, too. Plains Indians of North America wore wolf skins as disguises in order to be able to sneak up on bison they were hunting. Though currently the annual international trade is now only about 6,000-7,000 pelts, wolf fur can represent a substantial amount of income for some people. In addition, wolf meat is a prized part of the diet in some parts of the world. Like dog meat, which is commonly eaten in portions of Asia, wolf meat is eaten in winter and supposedly provides great benefits in keeping warm. After I gave a talk about wolves and wolf biology to Mongolian park guards several years ago, the first question I was asked was "How do wolves in North America taste?" Wolves also have been shot for sport, often after being chased by coursing hounds, on snow mobile, or even from an airplane. They are valued as trophies that can end up as rugs or wall hangings.

Wolves, unfortunately, kill domestic livestock. The domestication of animals some 12,000 years ago changed human views of wolves. As soon as wolves started killing sheep and goats, people's livelihoods and their ability to survive was threatened. To a large extent, the increase in numbers of domestic livestock paralleled the decrease in wolves' natural prey. Also, the selective breeding that made domestic animals easier to herd also eliminated much of their natural defensive behavior, and made them easy prey for wolves. As a result, much more effort was made to eliminate wolves from areas where livestock was being raised. Various cultures have carried out wolf control to differing degrees. In parts of southern Europe and Asia some wolves have always remained and people have tolerated them to some extent. However, this contrasts with the complete elimination of wolves on the British Isles, and the 300-year war on wolves that took place after European colonization of the United States that virtually eliminated 95% of wolves south of Canada.

The role livestock currently plays in the diets of wolves varies, as does the economic impact of depredations. This variation is reflected in human attitudes towards wolves. Although wolves eat every kind of livestock available to them, most livestock losses to wolves in Eurasia are of sheep. Where both species are available in Finland, wolves kill more sheep than cattle, and in India, more goats than sheep. Sheep are also the preferred prey in Poland and Italy. Depredations in Europe may be higher in general because in some places wolves have been able to survive by subsisting on human refuse and carrion, as well as livestock. The total economic loss in some areas can be high; in Tuscany, Italy, annual compensation for wolf and dog depredations averaged US$345,000, and in Spain annual payments averaged US$1-1.5 million. And overall, this threat

of loss moves thousands of livestock owners to loathe the idea wolves living on or near their properties.

Most losses in North America are of cattle and turkeys, only because relatively few sheep are raised where there are wolves. Based on availability, however, sheep are selected more often than cattle. In no area of North America are wolves mostly dependent on livestock, and only a tiny proportion of livestock owners ever have losses. Even though compensation paid for losses in the U.S. has only averaged about US$40,000 each year for the past 20 years, livestock losses can be very significant to those few farmers who lose animals.

One aspect of wolf depredation that many people are unaware of is that wolves kill dogs wherever the two species occur. In part this relates to the behavioral antagonism that wolves show towards all other canids, including other wolf packs. In some areas, however, wolves are an important food of wolves. Whatever the motivation, wolves appear to limit the number of stray dogs in Russia, and a survey in Croatia indicated that dogs were killed more often than any other domestic animal. In Wisconsin, U.S., compensation paid for wolf-killed hunting dogs has exceeded that paid for all other livestock. For some people, the monetary loss is much less than the emotional loss for a beloved pet, and it is easy to understand negative feelings toward wolves when pets are killed.

Other Reactions to Wolf Depredation

It should be emphasized that not all "troublesome" wolves are killed; some people's attitudes are such that if other means to reduce depredation are effective, they chose these as an alternative. A variety of non-lethal control methods have been tried and are being used to help prevent depredation by wolves on livestock. One of the oldest and most effective means is the use of guard animals, particularly dogs, but also llamas and donkeys. Dogs are most beneficial when used in combination with shepherds, and are common in parts of Europe, especially with flocks of sheep. Other techniques have been tried and used with some success, but none are consistently effective; these include the use of lights, sirens, flagging, propane exploders, and pyrotechnics. Livestock have been fitted with collars filled with toxic, noxious substances; the idea is that any wolf biting into such a collar and receiving a mouthful of sickening liquid will not do it again, regardless of whether an animal has a collar or not. Wolves also are trapped or captured by helicopter and relocated to new areas, but such animals usually roam widely and have been known to continue their depredating ways even years later.

Various animal husbandry methods have been correlated with preventing depredations, and often changing techniques can reduce damage by wolves. Livestock is least vulnerable to wolves when in open pastures or areas with reduced cover, and when not left in remote areas without tending by herders. Losses to wolves are reduced when calving or lambing areas are close to dwellings, and when newborns are held for some time before turning them loose in pastures. Some fences help reduce loss to predators, as does proper disposal of livestock carcasses (e.g., burying or burning them) so that wolves don't learn to scavenge them.

Financial compensation to livestock producers provides some sense of economic replacement, and may be the only means by which some people can justify allowing wolves in some areas. Without concomitant management of wolves or livestock, however, such compensation can end up being an unending obligation that does nothing more than subsidize old habits of livestock and wolf management, much to the chagrin of taxpayers.

Myths, Legends, and Stories

One characteristic of the relationships between wolves and humans is that the experiences make good stories, often so entertaining or fascinating that they have been passed on for generations. Whether truthful or embellished, these stories play an integral part of some cultures, and still influence opinions and attitudes of people today in the forms of myths and legends. For example, there are several universal images of wolves in the minds of many Westerners, scenes of which many know from stories they have heard read to them or seen in a painting. One depicts a bitterly cold winter night, and a Russian family thickly bundled under furs in a horse-drawn sled or troika racing across the snow; the mother and children are looking back over their shoulders, terrified, at a huge pack of ravenous wolves relentlessly chasing after them. This image certainly elicits and reinforces the fear of wolves. Another, however, is that of a lone wolf on a ridge top, silhouetted by the moon, howling a mournful song to his pack, future mate, or the world at large. This scene may invoke a feeling of peacefulness and yearning for a simpler relationship to the natural world.

Wolves are such a rich source of myth and legend because all early peoples in the northern half of the world had to coexist with them in some way. The powerful nature of these experiences have persisted in myths and stories that portray wolves in a positive or negative light.

Hunting and gathering cultures, such as those of most Native American peoples, likely had a healthy admiration for wolves. Wolves are proficient hunters, and thus often became totems of human groups or clans; that is, respected, spiritual animal representations of a family line. Ceremonies intended to maintain group cohesion or togetherness (sociality being a major characteristic of wolves) often involved human portrayals of wolf totems, often including the wearing of masks and pelts. Medicine men of a variety of tribes wore wolf skins in order to mimic the powers of wolves. Giant totem poles carved from individual trees often were centerpieces of communities. The survival skills of wolves often ended up as legends, as well, including an Eskimo story of an abandoned old woman forced to survive on her own who eventually turned into a wolf.

In Eurasia, early peoples dependent on hunting also admired and tried to emulate the wolf. Warrior peoples like early Germanics and Anglo-Saxons associated themselves with noble characteristics of wolves and portrayed the wolf on battle flags. The Ainu people of Japan believed in a protective wolf spirit. During the Middle Ages, people also ascribed magical powers to wolves; birth pains could be eased with powdered wolf liver, and a wolf's paw tied around the neck could relieve a sore throat. In some cultures, wolves were portrayed as collectors and distributors of information and knowledge; in others, they were known as fertility gods. One of the best-known legends related to wolf fertility is that of Romulus and Remus, twin sons of a vestal virgin who were banished to the wilderness. They were suckled and raised by wolves before being rescued and going on to become the legendary founders of Rome. Numerous other stories of "wolf children" have been recorded over the centuries, including Rudyard Kipling's Mowgli.

On the other hand, wolves have often been portrayed in a negative light. The advent of Christianity gave rise to the notion of humans as masters and not part of the natural world. In the Bible, wolves are portrayed as symbols of rapacity, wantonness, cunning, and deceit as related to human behavior, and came to be viewed as evil and threatening to the Roman Catholic Church. The subsequent legends of were-wolves, in particular, reinforced negative views of wolves. There were, in fact, demented or depraved persons who acted "were-wolfish", or lycanthropic, and their acts may have seemed magical or supernatural to the unaware. Stories of such people flourished and became engrained in the cultural imagination.

Wolves are consistently depicted as ferocious and sly. They are often used as metaphors for human behaviour, and appear in fairy tales or folk tales as a vehicle for moral teachings The story of the *Three Little Pigs* seems to suggest that adequate preparation against adversity is a good idea. In *Little Red Riding Hood*, keeping to the path and never being distracted from or interrupted in accomplishing one's task will probably result in coming to no harm. This is especially true when the distraction has sexual overtones as suggested by the identification of lusting human males as real "wolves", often giving wolf whistles to passing women. Aesop's tale of the wolf and the crane, where the crane's reward for removing a bone stuck in a wolf's throat is simply not to be eaten by the wolf, may give pause to do-gooders who expect rewards for every act of kindness. Finally, St. Francis' taming of the terrorizing wolf of Gubbio demonstrated to the local people the power and providence of the living God.

In post-colonial America, settlers brought with them a stereotypical, negative view of wolves, and transferred their fear and hatred of wolves to the challenges of the New World environment. Taming the wilderness was no less a passion than was eradicating wolves, and both seemed essential to advance civilization. Wolves were not considered an appropriate part of nature in the American West, and by the beginning of the 20th century, long after wolves in much of Europe had been exterminated, the federal government waged a campaign that rid even Yellowstone National Park of wolves. Not until the 1930s and 1940s were wolves even deemed worthy of scientific study, and not until the environmental movement of the 1970s did the public's attitude towards wolves begin to change in the U.S.

So what about the troika and wolf chases, or wolves howling at the moon? Are these, and other wolf stories, based on true depictions of wolf behavior, or are they simply distorted human perceptions brought to life through word or picture? Wolves certainly do chase and kill large mammals, sometimes even people, but only rabid wolves would probably have pursued a troika, and such an occurrence would have been rather rare. Wolves do howl at night, but no more so during the full moon than at other times of the month. All in all, many of the myths

Historically, many cultures have positively valued wolves, in large part because of wolf hunting prowess and survival skills.
Current-day humans also value these characteristics; in addition, many feel an affiliation with the social organization of wolves or perceive
an association of wolves with wilderness areas. Humans' close relationship with dogs also seems to affect feelings towards wolves.

The Recovery of Wolves in the American West

The above map shows the recent changes in the abundance and distribution of wolf packs that are recolonizing Yellowstone National Park, USA, and the surrounding areas (approximate centers of pack territories indicated). These changes follow the reintroduction of 31 wolves during 1995 and 1996.

One of the remarkable wolf conservation success stories is occurring in the American West. Yellowstone National Park was established in 1872, before any other such park worldwide, and is one of the great natural areas of the world. Early on, however, Park policy included predator control, and by 1926 there were no wolf packs left. Decades later, Park officials, the scientific community, and the general public came to realize the importance of the wolf as part of a naturally functioning ecosystem. Years of scientific and public planning and input resulted in a call for restoring wolves to the Park, with a good understanding of the possible consequences of such an effort on the fauna within and around the park, and on the people who live near and visit the Park. As a result, several packs of wolves were captured in Alberta, Canada, both during winter 1995 (14 individuals) and 1996 (17 individuals), held in acclimation pens in the Park for 10 weeks, and then released. By the end of winter 1996, the released wolves had settled into 9 different packs, all but 2 mostly within the Park, with a total of 51 individuals in the population. Since then, the wolf population has increased steadily in both numbers and distribution. By 2002, 31 packs and a total of 272 individuals made up a population that ranged up to 80 km (50 mi) from the Park borders; in fact, more than half the packs resided outside of the Park. This means that the population grew in numbers more than 5-fold in 6 years (a rate of increase of 32% per year), and approximately tripled the area over which they roamed. Since the reintroduction, wolves have caused some livestock damage, but Yellowstone National Park is now the premier viewing area for wolves in North America.

and legends we know of are probably based in part on real attributes of wolves, but most certainly have interwoven a number of human characteristics, both good and bad, that make us feel even more connected to a powerful and remarkable animal.

Contemporary Human Values and Attitudes

Some of the long-held values we humans have had concerning wolves still persist. We still believe, or at a minimum are subtly influenced by, the myths and stories that have been passed on for generations. But in addition to fearing wolves as killers, despising them as depredators and a "threat" to big game populations, and valuing them as commodities and objects of sport, attitudes towards wolves have increased in variety, just as our cultures, technologies, and living styles have expanded and diversified.

Negative

One relatively new fear is that of land-use restrictions resulting from the legal protection of wolves. If logging or even recreational hiking can't go on in some areas because wolves are denning nearby, if livestock grazing on government land is restricted because of the potential presence of recolonizing wolves, or if areas are closed to big game hunting because they are deemed necessary to ensure success of wolf reintroductions, then many people see wolves as obstacles and detriments to the kind of life they wish to lead.

Some wolf management activities have become the symbols of big government and control by people living far away from where the effects of such rulemaking are most heavily felt. As a consequence, wolves are seen as the cause of unnecessary and undesirable changes.

Also, some people dislike wolves because it costs too much to manage them. The idea that tax money pays for managers to reintroduce, protect, regulate the harvest of, and in reaction to

Many people like the idea of protecting and even restoring wolves to public lands such as here in Yellowstone National Park, but the fear of government restrictions on the use of private lands turns others against such conservation efforts.

depredations, turn around and kill wolves may seem just plain wrong. Without wolves, no compensation payments would have to be made for livestock losses, and more revenue from recreational hunting may be forthcoming. Wolves are, indeed, an expensive proposition in some places, and many people don't like paying for them.

Positive

Many people are infatuated with or simply like and respect wolves. To be sure, there is a cultural value of wolves as symbols of hunting prowess and family life. Wolves are respected as a species of survivors with many abilities and traits that are valued by humans. But along with this respect and feeling of affinity for wolves, they also are valued aesthetically. Humans find wolves attractive to look at; their size, form, and varied coloration are appealing. This is not surprising, given the number of pet dogs that live in the world. But perhaps most importantly, wolves also have come to represent wilderness and ecosystem integrity. This value likely results, in part, from the fact that only relatively recently were wolves in North America eliminated from all but wilderness-type areas, and many people don't realize how adaptable they have become elsewhere in the world. But in yearning for places relatively unaffected by humans, areas with wolves seem to meet an important wilderness criterion for many people.

There is a recent recognition that removing major parts of ecosystems significantly changes their workings. One of the most persuasive arguments for restoring wolves to Yellowstone National Park was that wolves were the only species that was present at the time of European colonization of North America but that was missing from the Park; restoring them would not only complete the list of fauna, but also help correct the affects of over-browsing by elk, and the "imbalance" of the rest of the plant and animal community. In this case, wolves were valued an essential part of an ecosystem, as well as acting as a symbol of righting the wrongs of the past.

In addition to valuing wolves as a product (e.g., coats, trophies), they also are sometimes captured, raised, and kept as "pets" by individuals. More often they are interbred with dogs to supposedly end up with a somewhat more tractable canid with the looks of a wolf. In either case such use is a bad idea – neither make good pets and may end up injuring or killing someone. More

often than not, such animals are kept in circumstances not the least bit similar to what a wolf in the wild needs or should have.

Wolves recently have been marketed as a draw for tourism and recreation. Economic analyses suggest that millions of new dollars have flowed into the economies of the states in the Rocky Mountains of the U.S. where wolves have been reintroduced because of the appeal to tourists of being in "wolf country" and maybe even catching a glimpse of a wolf. Wolves are rare enough to see that even Alaska has drawn tourists by advertising itself as a "Serengeti of the North", offering majestic and abundant wildlife interacting in the ways they have done so for thousands of years. In addition, the variety of other positive values of wolves has resulted in a boom in the marketing of wolf paraphernalia (e.g., t-shirts, mugs, rugs, paintings, note cards, photos, videotapes, and even books).

Finally, wolves have been valued in a cynical sort of way as political and strategic tools. As endangered species, some people view wolves as potentially helping to protect both large and small areas from timber harvesting, development, aerial over-flights of military planes, noisy recreational uses, etc. Often wolves themselves are not the focus of a given environmental protection effort, but a means by which a situation can be better exploited to achieve some end other than conservation of wolves. For example, people who don't like military aircraft flying over their cabins may claim that endangered wolves are being disturbed by these flights (but they're not) and ask the military to change the flight paths. Wolves also are used extensively in funding-raising for environmentally oriented organizations and groups, some of which actually do a tremendous amount to help conserve wolves, but others that just know a good marketing tool when they see one.

From all these examples, it should be easy to see why the interactions of humans and wolves have resulted in the wolf being one of the most hated and, at the same time, the most admired animals in the world.

Conservation:
The Future of Wolf Populations

Humans have managed wolves for a long time. Whether by killing individual wolves that attacked themselves or their livestock, or by digging into dens to kill whole litters of pups, prehistoric and contemporary humans purposefully have tried to affect the number and distribution of wolves for their own benefit. Now, however, many people question or oppose such persecution, or even the regulated harvest and specifically directed control of wolves. This change in attitude is due in large part to increased knowledge of wolves. In addition to ongoing worries about wolf predation, wolf conservation has become an ecological and ethical concern, and much time and effort has gone into trying to figure out how wolves and humans can continue to co-exist.

Changes in Attitudes and Knowledge

Historically, attitudes towards wolves, if they changed, went from good to bad. Someone not directly affected by wolves might have some cultural or mystical idea of them that was positive, or at least might think them benign. But with the loss of a domestic animal or, worse yet, an attack on an acquaintance or oneself, wolves would become feared and/or hated in an instant. On the other hand, wolves themselves couldn't do much to promote their image, or get it changed to a positive one. Wolf advocacy has come about as the result of several key events.

The change in our perception of wolves has to do with the advancement of scientific management of wildlife, with the development of a land ethic, and with the discovery that humans were causing self-destructive effects on the environment. In the U.S., Aldo Leopold wrote the first professional guidelines for wildlife management in 1933, and Sigurd Olson and Adolph Murie were the first scientists to quantitatively record their observations of wolves in Minnesota and Alaska, respectively, during the late 1930s and early 1940s. These studies profoundly changed Olson's own beliefs and perceptions of wolves, once seeing them as "murderous" and "marauders", but subsequently as "an integral part of the wilderness community". In addition to Leopold's innovative suggestion in 1944 to restore wolves to Yellowstone National Park, his other landmark contribution was the publication of *A Sand County Almanac* in 1949 in which he poetically and convincingly set forth a land ethic that encompassed the stewardship of wildlife as well. Upon reflection of his earlier experiences with wolves and deer in the American Southwest, Leopold wrote "Only the mountain has lived long enough to listen objectively to the howl of a wolf". In 1962, Rachel Carson published *Silent Spring*, a disturbing yet enlightening account of the effects of pesticides on the environment, in which she called for a change in the way humankind viewed the natural world.

By the mid-1960s, wolf populations throughout the world were at their nadir. Attitudes were changing, however, such that bounties on predators in the U.S. were being eliminated, the concept of endangered species was established, and wolves became one of the first species to receive federal protection under the new endangered species act. With these actions, the historic fate of the wolf and many other species was reconsidered, and conservation efforts were begun to counter past practices. Similar transformations in attitudes also occurred in Europe, where by the 1970s wolf conservation programs were also beginning.

The pace of wolf science also accelerated in the 1960s, particularly with the advent of radio telemetry (small transmitters on collars that allowed scientists to locate wolves almost at will). In the 1970s, knowledge of wolves, particularly those that lived in the forests of Europe and North America, increased rapidly, as did the number of biologists studying wolves. The result was that by

1996, there were over 2,500 scientific articles published about wolves, and stacks of scientific books about them.

In the past 30 years, the proportion of people with favorable views of the wolf have increased tremendously, and millions of dollars have been spent on wolf research, management, promotion, and recovery. Although attitudes toward wolves in parts of Europe have improved most in cities, strong feelings against them prevail in many rural areas. Even though people in rural Sweden and Norway want the wolf to survive, most reindeer owners and farmers are against wolf protection. In Scotland, most people are not in favor of wolf reintroduction; this has not been the case in the Midwest and West of the U.S. where a majority of the local public either supported wolf restoration or at least did not oppose it. In parts of Canada and the U.S., attitudes are related to gender (females = +), education level (more = +), age (younger = +), knowledge of wolves (lower = +), size of community (larger = +), level of fear of wolves (lower = +), big game hunting experience (less = +), and location with respect to wolves (farther = +). In general, farmers and ranchers, a small proportion of the population, have the most negative views of wolves. In contrast, urban residents, one of the most numerous demographic groups, as well as members of environmental organizations, have the most positive and protectionist attitudes.

One unintended consequence of efforts to protect and restore wolves has been what some people consider the "over-promotion" of wolves. In order to change opinions, a new mythology of wolves evolved in which the evil, overabundant wolf was transformed into the unfairly persecuted, endangered wolf. Wolves became good, not bad, and the problems they caused were due to people, not some inherent trait of wolves. Wolves evolved into symbols of wilderness, of nature at its best, of an environment that was functioning as it was meant to. Scientific knowledge about wolves had increased, but public knowledge of wolves was limited and often wrong. Wolves did cause some problems, and dealing with them was difficult. In places where wolf recovery seemed to be gaining success, wolf conservationists realized that, in the long run, a more balanced view of wolves was essential. The real possibility of an overpopulation of wolves suggested that a backlash of opinion was possible, and that many more people might see wolves in a different light if problems (e.g., livestock depredation) increased dramatically. This concern emphasized the need for a broad approach to wolf conservation that included consideration of a number of approaches, including occasional wolf control.

Conservation Needs

The basic tenet of wolf conservation is that wolves have a right to exist in a wild state in viable populations. There are few places on earth, however, where humans do not affect wolves (and vice versa) in some way, and thus wolf-human interactions are a principal focus of wolf conservation. To address these interactions, and in particular the conservation threats to wolves, a variety of needs must be met. Conservation actions must build on what we already know about wolves and humans, and are essential to achieve the goal of long-term coexistence.

Biological

Any assessment of wolf population viability needs to include some estimate of population size and change. Wolves are notoriously difficult to census in areas without snow cover, and although radio-telemetry has been extremely useful for counting wolves in relatively small areas, estimating numbers within populations and detecting other than major changes in abundance over large areas are difficult. A variety of methods have been used around the world to assess wolf numbers, including questionnaires, field observations, trends in prey numbers, snow tracking, howling, counts of scats, and aerial surveys. Most often, reasonably derived

counts in specific areas are extrapolated to larger areas in which relative abundances of wolves have been determined. Because of the resilience of most wolf populations, exact counts are not as important to conservation as is consistent monitoring to assess presence and trends.

The relatively new field of molecular ecology will, in time, allow more specific assessment of the genetic status of populations. Genetic sampling of wolves can be done non-invasively (e.g., by analyzing DNA on scats) and the results can tell the degree of inbreeding in a population, and the extent to which small populations are isolated from other wolves. Such results, along with geographic analyses of wolf distribution, can help in identifying conservation units within which specific management options can be implemented. For example, such assessments of an introduced population that began with 4 or 5 genetically unrelated wolves could indicate how much each of these wolves had participated in breeding. If only 2 or 3 had done most of the reproduction, additional wolves from elsewhere might be added to the population to increase the genetic diversity.

The assessment of habitat suitability for wolves is an ongoing process because changes in the landscape will continue to occur. Monitoring the number and distribution of ungulates is a primary focus because of the close relationship between wolf numbers and the relative abundance of food. In some circumstances, habitat improvement through prey reintroductions is an important means to assure the viability of wolf populations; red deer and roe deer have both been reintroduced into Italy and Portugal to help sustain wolves. Human activities also affect the distribution and abundance of wolves, whether directly by killing wolves or indirectly by eliminating prey. New models of wolf habitat quality incorporate these and other factors to derive maps of the relative suitability of landscapes for wolves, and also for the places that can serve as corridors connecting wolf populations.

Legal

The legal status of wolves among the countries where they are found varies from complete protection to unlimited and unregulated harvested. Many countries, such as those in Europe and North America, have signed international agreements related to wolf conservation, and have drafted local, national, and/or collaborative international plans and treaties to assure coordinated management of wolves. Others, such as the new republics in Central Asia, have given little attention to wolves because they either have not had the motivation to spend time and money in developing long-term strategies, or do not see that such efforts would be fruitful or useful.

The most planning and protection usually involves the zoning of areas within which the most appropriate management strategies can be implemented. They often include refugia for wolves; that is, places of complete protection where wolf populations can thrive and often provide the sources of wolves that make adjacent areas suitable enough for wolves. Examples include national parks, refuges, and wilderness areas. In many areas, legal harvest of wolf populations are an important component because 1) such activity (if properly planned and regulated) rarely has any long-term negative effect on a wolf population, and 2) it can provide an inexpensive means to keep wolf numbers, and thus wolf conflicts with humans, from escalating. Where such public harvest is socially unacceptable, government agencies often play the role of wolf population managers and remove depredating wolves as is done in the Great Lakes area of the United States.

A major problem in enforcing the legal protection of wolves is that illegal killing of wolves is sometimes ignored. When regulations seem unreasonable to local people, and this is often the case when a majority of people from outside of a wolf-inhabited area decide on wolf management regulations, a policy of benign neglect may follow. Enforcement officials "look the other way" when wolves are killed in defense of property, or in

anticipation of such problems, or simply when they seem too common for the local good. Such inaction indicates that management plans have not been fully justified and accepted, and that additional efforts need to be made to reach a consensus.

Wolf Management

The two most important aspects of wolf management are reducing conflicts with humans and achieving recovery of wolf populations in suitable areas where they have been extirpated. Wolf management is needed where there are either too many or too few wolves, respectively. Where there are few conflicts and wolf numbers seem adequate for population persistence, less management is needed.

Many utilitarian and economic conflicts with wolves center on their effects on wild ungulates (and thus the opportunities for humans to hunt them), and with livestock depredation. Wild ungulates are among the most managed wildlife because they are such an important game species. Keeping populations high but slightly below the carrying capacity of their habitat is a central focus for agencies and governments delegated to manage ungulates for human recreation and subsistence. As a result, prey management for wolves has more to do with adjusting the human harvest of ungulates in a way that supplements those killed by wolves than it does with manipulating habitats. The harvest by humans can be adjusted by limiting the times people can hunt, the number of animals they can kill, and the access to hunting areas. Often, a regulated wolf harvest is established not to necessarily reduce wolf predation in a significant way, but rather to appease local people who perceive that wolves are "robbing" them of opportunity and would otherwise illegally kill wolves in response to perceived overprotection.

The keys to managing livestock depredation at an acceptable level involve three components. First, adequate steps must be taken to prevent depredations from occurring, including animal husbandry practices that are effective and use of deterrents, such as guard animals. In addition, compensation payments for losses where livestock producers have tried prevention techniques, or incentives to producers to try new techniques, can be important conservation initiatives. Finally, allowances for the removal of specific wolves causing repeated damage need to be in place.

Where wolf recovery is desired and biologically feasible, the

most important concern seems to be the source of repopulating wolves. In most places, public sentiment is much more in favor of naturally recolonizing wolves (e.g., from Italy to France, Poland to Germany, Canada to the U.S.) than they are of translocated wolves. This preference has been revealed both through attitude surveys and through the public's actions (i.e., rapid killing of wolves) in response to translocation efforts. Even under circumstances where the recolonizing wolves maintain fully protected status, local residents prefer natural changes rather than government-assisted ones.

The circumstances where translocated wolves (e.g., to Idaho and Yellowstone National Park in the U.S.), and even captive wolves (e.g., Mexican wolves to the southwestern U.S.), have been reintroduced with partial or total success where no nearby source population of wolves is available for natural recolonization. There seem to be little problems either with wolves adjusting to new areas, regardless of release technique (e.g., "slow", after some initial acclimation in pens vs. immediate), or with the success of properly maintained captive bred animals learning to live in wild settings. In either case, detailed planning and biological assessments are required to maximize chances of success. In the United States, some releases have been given special legal designation as an "experimental" population; such classification allows management options like capture and removal, that otherwise would not have been allowed with naturally recolonizing, fully protected wolves. Public acceptance also has been increased by assuring that losses of domestic animals will be fully compensated.

Human Management

Wolf conservation is necessarily a complicated endeavor. It involves the careful and long-term coordination of expertise from a variety of sources, as well as consideration of the values and attitudes of the people that governments are obliged to represent. Perhaps the most important consideration is the role that public opinion plays in wolf conservation. Government managers are public servants, and they must strive to implement the best possible actions based on science and the public's understanding of the issues. To this end, various methods for obtaining public input to management plans have been tried. Public information meetings, distribution of education materials, and allowing for public representation on policy councils or in roundtable meetings all can serve to have an informed public help determine the goals of wolf conservation.

The efforts to educate the general public about wolves is not easy because some beliefs are so closely held (see Chapter 10). Also, prejudice and ignorance abound not only in the general public, but sometimes in governments, and in both anti-wolf and pro-wolf non-governmental organizations, as well. No one solution will work for all conservation efforts. In fact, every case has specific differences that make it unique. As a result, education efforts can give general facts about wolf ecology and behavior, the likely outcome of management options, and perhaps some sense of the social and economic costs and benefits of conserving wolves, but these just cannot be definitive for every situation.

The contentious nature of wolf conservation is due to the widely and often deeply held beliefs of many citizens, so education efforts are critical components of all wolf conservation efforts. Personal contacts and interactions often seem more effective than written materials or other impersonal media messages. Certainly, appropriate information presented in schools or at workshops for people of all ages is useful. Many people are so visually oriented now that well-written and produced videos can provide straightforward and simple information that will help the public understand the underlying biology of wolves and the basis of the wide-ranging values and attitudes that are the essential components of wolf conservation.

The solution to achieving viable populations of wolves throughout their historic range is not just to "leave them alone" in remote, unpopulated areas, but to work at figuring out how wolves and people can co-exist in ways that are mutually compatible. Wolves are a species with tremendous flexibility and talents for survival. They have found many ways to exist environments as different as the desert and the Arctic tundra. They are resilient, adaptable, resourceful, and capable of coexisting with other competing predators. Such characteristics seem both admirable and of the utmost importance for survival. Perhaps we should reflect on their abilities a little more often, then roll up our sleeves and get to the business of taking care of ourselves and of one of the most charismatic creatures that has ever lived, to the betterment of both.

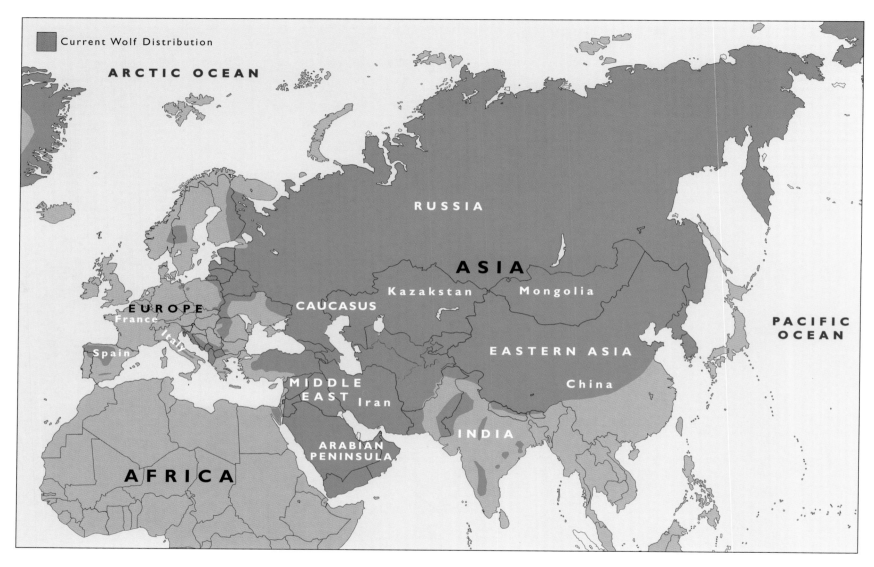

In Eurasia, the subspecies scientifically identified as Canis lupus albus *is found throughout the Old World Arctic.*
C. l. arabs *is amongst the smallest of wolves and inhabits the Arabian Peninsula. The wide-ranging* C. l. communis *subspecies lives*
in the boreal forest and adjacent areas of Northcentral Russia. C. l. cubanensis *is a type that is found in the Caucasus region, and* C. l. italicus
has a limited distribution on the Italian Peninsula. C. l. lupaster *is found in northeast Africa (Egypt) and adjacent Middle East,* C. l. pallipes
occurs from the Middle East to India, and C. l. lupus *is the wolf known throughout Europe, Central and Eastern Asia.*

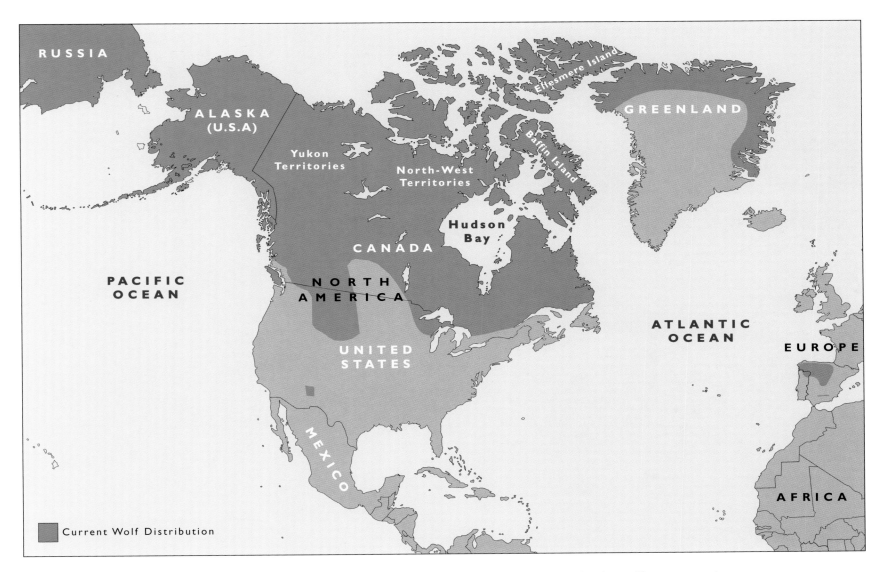

Current Wolf Distribution

In North America, Canis lupus arctos , also referred to as the Arctic or Tundra wolf, ranges on the borders of Greenland and across the Canadian Arctic. C. l. baileyi, known as the Mexican wolf, occurs as a recovering population in the southwest U.S. and Mexico. The Eastern timber wolf, C. l. lycaon, ranges across eastern North America, while C. l. nubilus occurs in east-central Canada and central and Western U.S. and C. l. occidentalis is numerous in Alaska and northwest Canada.

Wolf Facts

Classification

Class: Mammalia
Order: Carnivora
Family: Canidae
Genus: *Canis*
Scientific Name: *Canis lupus*
Currently classified into 13 subspecies
Common Names (including regional or subspecific names): gray wolf, common wolf, grey wolf, timber wolf, plains wolf, Arctic wolf, tundra wolf, steppe wolf, Mexican wolf, Tibetan wolf, Iberian wolf, buffalo wolf, lobo (Spanish), loup (French), wolf (German), lupo (Italian), varg (Swedish).

Average Body Size and Structure

Total Length:
Males　　　　150-200 cm (60-78 in)
Females　　　140-185 cm (55-72 in)

Shoulder Height:　　65-80 cm (26-32 in)

Weight:
Males　　　　43-48 kg (95-105 lb)
Females　　　36-42 kg (80-90 lb)

Wolves in the southern parts of their range are generally smaller than those in the north.

Life History Traits and Ecology

Gestation Period:　　　61-64 days

Litter Size:　　　1-11, usually 4-6

Age at Dispersal:　　5-60 months, usually 20-26 months

Maximum Life Span: 12 years in the wild

Prey Requirements (no./wolf/year): approximately 15-19 adult white-tailed deer, or 16 adult cow caribou, or 4 adult and 5 calf moose each year.

Acknowledgments

A number of people are responsible for giving me the opportunities and encouragement to study and write about wolves. Dave Mech first gave me the opportunity to be a summer intern in northeastern Minnesota, howling and trapping with Fred Harrington; Steve Fritts let me spend a summer getting essential practical experience with him in northwestern Minnesota; Lloyd Keith took me on as a graduate student to work in northeastern Alberta and turned me into a scientist; Bill Berg was a most helpful colleague when I began my work in northcentral Minnesota; and Luigi Boitani offered me international insights and inspirations. I am most grateful to them all for their friendship, guidance, and mentorship.

The opportunity to author this book is a result of a generous suggestion by David Macdonald. To write it, I have drawn heavily from the most recent summaries of wolf information presented in *Wolves: behavior, ecology and conservation* edited by Dave Mech and Luigi Boitani. In that book, numerous colleagues and I worked hard to present the most up-to-date technical knowledge available concerning wolves, and they all allowed me to preview and freely relate their findings. These wonderful and generous friends include, in alphabetical order, Cheryl Asa, Warren Ballard, Luigi Boitani, Lu Carbyn, Jean Cochrane, Paolo Ciucci, Steve Fritts, Fred Harrington, Bob Hayes, Gary Henry, Brian Kelly, Terry Kreeger, Dave Mech, Ron Nowak, Jane Packard, Rolf Peterson, Mike Phillips, Doug Smith, Bob Stephenson, Carles Vila, and Bob Wayne. I also have read much of what many other people have written about wolves in a variety of ways, and I am sure that I have been influenced by, and now pass on, many of their insights and thoughts.

Though I assume full responsibility for any errors or lapses in critical thinking presented in this book, I am very grateful to Dick DeGraaf for reading the entire draft and providing innumerable editorial suggestions that only a good friend can make. I also thank Bill Grohmann for providing much-needed moral support. My brother, Mark, has always had a big influence on what I do and accomplish, as have my mother, Edith, and late father, Don; I thank them each for their encouragement throughout my life. Finally, my deepest thanks are to Susan and Mollie, my wife and daughter, for their good-natured tolerance, joyful companionship, and unremitting love.

Map information on page 114 provided by Douglas W. Smith and Debra Guernsey, Yellowstone National Park, USA.

Maps on page 128-129 adapted from: Mech, L. D., and L. Boitani. 2004. Grey wolf (Canis lupus). In Sillero-Zubiri, C., M. Hoffmann and D.W. Macdonald (eds). Canids: foxes, wolves, jackals and dogs. Status survey and conservation action plan. IUCN/SSC Canid Specialist Group. Gland, Switzerland.

Index

Recommended Reading

Mech, L. D., and L. Boitani, eds. 2003. *Wolves: Behavior, Ecology and Conservation.* University of Chicago Press, Chicago, Illinois, USA. (Read this and you will know as much about wolves as almost anyone else.)

Sillero-Zubirir, C., M. Hoffmann, and D W. Macdonald, eds. 2004. *Canids: Foxes, Wolves, Jackals and Dogs.* Status survey and conservation action plan. IUCN/SSC Canid specialist Group. Gland, Switzerland.

Some International Agencies Supporting Wolf Conservation

Large Carnivore Initiative for Europe: http://large-carnivores-lcie.org/index.htm

The International Wolf Center, Ely Minnesota, USA: www.wolf.org

The World Conservation Union (IUCN), Species Survival Commission, Wolf Specialist Group and Canid Specialist Group (http://www.canids.org/), Gland, Switzerland; http://www.iucn.org/themes/ssc/sgs/sgs.htm